The Tibetan
Art of
Serenity

Also by Christopher Hansard

The Tibetan Art of Positive Thinking
The Tibetan Art of Living

The Tibetan
Art of
Serenity

HOW TO HEAL FEAR AND
GAIN CONTENTMENT

CHRISTOPHER
HANSARD

HODDER
MOBIUS

Copyright © 2006 by Christopher Hansard

First published in Great Britain in 2005 by Hodder & Stoughton
A division of Hodder Headline

A Mobius book

2

A CIP catalogue record for this title is available from the British Library

ISBN 0340835109

Typeset in Trump Mediaeval by Palimpsest Book Production Limited,
Polmont, Stirlingshire
Printed and bound in Great Britain
by Mackays of Chatham plc, Chatham, Kent

Hodder Headline's policy is to use papers that are natural, renewable
and recyclable products and made from wood grown in sustainable forests.
The logging and manufacturing processes are expected to conform to the
environmental regulations of the country of origin.

Hodder & Stoughton Ltd
A division of Hodder Headline
338 Euston Road
London NW1 3BH

To my life's journey

I would like to acknowledge the help and advice of
Caro Handley, Rowena Webb, Jacqui Lewis, Helen Coyle
and my agent Kay McCauley.

CONTENTS

Introduction

Fear is something all people have in common. Each of us, whatever our race or creed, know the anxiety, sense of foreboding and panic that fear engenders. Yet paradoxically, despite the universality of fear, when we are afraid, we feel isolated and alone, as though no one else can share in or understand what we are going through. That which we have in common with others is also what separates us from them when we need them most.

Fear is disempowering, spiritually and materially. Fear leads us to illness, conflict and unhappiness. It is through fear that we limit ourselves, telling ourselves that we can't have what we wish for, can't manage the job, relationship or challenge that would make us happy.

For most of us, fear becomes a habit very early in life. We believe it will always be with us and accept it as part of our burden. Yet each one of us is capable of living without fear. And a life without fear is a life transformed, for when we let go of fear, serenity takes its place. With serenity our inner chaos becomes still, we find inner balance, and we have the key to inner and outer transformation. We are able to think more clearly, make decisions more easily and experience love and contentment more fully. Life becomes a blessing.

Serenity is not something we have to acquire or reach for outside ourselves. It lies within each one of us, waiting to blossom. And it is through the skilful use of our own thought energy that we can discover and enjoy the serenity we have within.

The practitioners of the ancient Tibetan spiritual and religious discipline of Bön understood that the way we think affects everything we do. They taught that to create new ways of living and to become emotionally and spiritually rich, we must learn how to think skilfully. Most powerfully of all, they knew that understanding and transforming the nature of our own thought energy is the key to overcoming the greatest of all obstacles, fear.

Learning how to use thought skilfully is far simpler and more straightforward than you might imagine. In this book I will explain the nature of fear, the reasons for its power over us and the ways each of us may overcome and transform fear, choosing instead to live with serenity. I will offer practical and simple exercises, based on ancient Bön rituals, which will help you to take the journey from fear to serenity. Whatever your fears, however old, deep or strongly rooted, if you follow the guidance I offer, you will be able to transform your fears into the peace of mind, happiness and fulfilment that is serenity.

THE ORIGINS OF BÖN

Buddhism is the religion most closely associated with Tibet today. For 1,200 years, until the invasion of Tibet by China in 1959, Buddhism was the dominant religion in this beautiful, mountainous country. Yet many years before the advent of Buddhism, Bön was the system of cultural and spiritual teaching in Tibet. For 17,000 years Bön was predominant in Central Asia and Tibet and, though it later gave way to Buddhism, there remained many thousands, in Tibet and elsewhere around the world, who followed the teachings of Bön.

When Buddhism supplanted Bön during a time of social unrest in Tibet, the two religions coexisted peacefully for some years. Only later, when some Buddhists began to persecute the Bön community, did Bön take on some of the trappings of Buddhism. From this developed Reformed Bön, whose followers are known as Bön-pos.

However, despite the emergence of Reformed Bön, the original Bön teachings, known as the Bön of the Ngagpas, remained very much alive. This is the tradition in which I was trained, from the age of four, for twenty-three years.

My teacher, Ürgyen Nam Chuk, was a Ngagpa, a person of high spiritual calibre. The Ngagpas looked after their communities. They conducted weddings and funerals, dispensed justice and performed rituals for the protection and benefit of the community.

Ürgyen Nam Chuk came from the Nam or 'Sky' clan, famous for their medical skills, spiritual teachings and psychic powers. Almost thirty years before the invasion of Tibet by China a senior member of the Nam clan foresaw what would happen. The clan warned Tibet's leaders and then left the country, settling in various Indian cities. Some of the Ngagpas were chosen to travel to distant parts of the world, in search of those who could be trained to continue their teachings. Under the practices of Bön those of other races and cultures were not excluded from these teachings if they were spiritually and intellectually suitable. To find the chosen candidates, the Ngagpas used a complex and profound astrological system, which told them where in the world to go, as well as who they must look for.

This is how I came to meet my teacher. Ürgyen Nam Chuk was one of the Ngagpas sent out into the world to train others. It was in New Zealand, where my family had settled, that he approached my parents, introduced himself and explained that he represented a Tibetan spiritual tradition that had suggested, via an astrological system, that I might be a candidate for its teaching. My surprised parents agreed to meet Ürgyen again and, after a series of meetings, agreed that he might teach me, if it was what I wanted. I was happy to be taught by Ürgyen, having anticipated his arrival and recognised him as someone important in my life as soon as I saw him. My parents were aware of the tradition, common to Bön and Buddhism, of the reincarnation of spiritual teachers. But Ürgyen explained to them that I was not a reincarnated teacher but rather a person with special and particular abilities and a rare consciousness that needed training.

For the next twenty-three years he worked with me, always showing me patience, kindness, compassion and respect. I was never treated as special, simply as an ordinary boy who was also his pupil. I went to a normal school and did all the normal schoolboy things, but before and after school each day and on weekends and holidays I went to Ürgyen's house for my lessons. I became almost a part of Ürgyen's family – his wife, Tamdin, and his three children welcomed me and I loved being with them. Tamdin was from a famous family of Buddhist teachers, and the fact that Ürgyen and Tamdin were able to practise their religions side by side harmoniously for many years is confirmation of the common threads of Buddhism and Bön.

Of course there were times when, like any boy, I got fed up and skipped my lessons. But Ürgyen simply waited patiently for me to return, and I always did. Ürgyen's teaching was entirely by word of mouth. Nothing was ever written down; he simply explained what he knew and asked me to repeat it back to him. When I was a small child, his teachings and exercises were very simple. Later he taught me at a deeper and more profound level, testing me with oral examinations as well as waiting for me to experience physically what he taught, so that I knew it with my body as well as with my mind.

Ürgyen taught me the skills and beliefs as well as the mystery and wonder of Bön. Besides being a tantric yoga expert and a lama, or religious teacher, he was a physician of Bön medicine. He was also a shaman – not the kind who entered a trance after being 'overcome' by the gods but one who was trained in special knowledge and who was able to perform magic as a result. Ürgyen and the other Ngagpas were the Merlins of Tibet, mystical, magical healers and masters of miracles.

My education with Ürgyen lasted until I was twenty-seven, and soon after this he died. I felt his loss deeply, and for forty-nine days and nights I carried out the rituals appropriate to the passing of a master, at a consecrated place high on New Zealand's Pihanga Mountain. Eventually, now a Ngagpa myself, I walked the long path down the mountain, knowing that all was well but uncertain about the path I should follow in my own life.

Ürgyen had always made it clear that I must use the knowledge he had given me in the way that seemed right to me. For a few years I travelled, practising Tibetan medicine and waiting for the right direction to reveal itself. Finally, I came to Britain and established the Eden Medical Centre in London's King's Road, a healing centre to which people could come for their physical, spiritual and emotional care. In the centre I practise Tibetan medicine alongside a dedicated group of other complementary and orthodox health practitioners.

The Tibetan Art of Serenity addresses a particular aspect of human existence – our relationship with fear. The purpose of fear is to help us find a pathway to serenity. If we are willing, fear can be a guide and an ally in our journey of learning, at the end of which lies the true joy of serene living.

1

FREEDOM FROM FEAR

When you become free from fear, the benefits are many. You will discover in yourself the ability to form more satisfying relationships, commit more fully, love more deeply, understand your life with clarity and insight, and make wiser choices. Therefore your fear stands like a barrier between you and much that is good and valuable in your life. Those who are ruled by their fear mistrust, doubt, look for the negative in every situation and have clouded judgement. They are also closed, unable to accept love, abundance, joy and success, or to recognise what is good and worthwhile when it is offered to them.

With the absence of fear you can live your life as you choose, casting off restrictions and acting in harmony with others and the world around you. Problems and misfortunes will be unable to defeat you; you will approach them with the serenity that allows you to accept them and move on. You will be unaffected by changing fortunes, able to take all that comes in your stride and to bring benefit to yourself and to those around you, both family and community. When you release fear, your life becomes filled with pleasure at the joy of living. You gain powerful insight into the complex relationship between your inner and outer selves and you find the means to self-expression.

With freedom from fear you find that you are both ordinary and extraordinary. You become prepared to take risks, and you rise to the challenges in your life, while at the same time knowing when to let some pass by. In all the experiences and people that you meet in your life, you will find perpetual inspiration. Your humanity will grow, as will your insight and common sense. You will feel a responsibility to be compassionate and non-judgemental towards your fellow human beings. An unlimited and constant peace will always be with you. You will see the divine in all circumstances and in all people. Your sense of humour will increase, and your readiness to laugh at yourself will become part of the way you deal with the world.

The release from fear is like a spiritual earthquake, which will radically alter the course of your life. You may see things differently and choose new directions, and others may find you changed. But this change will be for the better, and you will never wish to go back to the way things were before.

THE BÖN VIEW OF FEAR

Generally people think of fear as the response to something threatening, such as bad news or danger. The threat may be immediate and obvious or more subtle and insidious. Fear may be our response to what we see as an overbearing person, a cruel god, a ruthless belief system or circumstances beyond our control.

In the Bön view, however, fear is seen not in terms of the perceived or imagined threat but in terms of the response it provokes in us. According to Bön, fear is any experience, physical, emotional, intellectual or spiritual, that creates powerful attachment, repulsion or a sense of powerlessness. So although the experiences that make us afraid may differ, the results within ourselves do not.

When we are in our mothers' womb we experience her fears. These are the lessons that we most need to learn to prepare us for the physical world we will face after birth, and it is therefore in the womb that we establish the patterns of our future fears. Because these fear patterns are so deep-rooted, taken in unconsciously along with the sustenance from our mothers, it requires the skilful use of conscious thought to begin to dislodge them.

Why do we experience fear? Because it is in fear itself that the path to serenity lies. Without fear to show us the way we would never learn the lessons of serenity. It is by going into the depths of fear that exist within our human consciousness that we find all that is needed to heal fear.

It is a commonly held view in the Western world that the best approach to fear is either to bury it or to face it head on, but these approaches are unwise. If you suppress fear, it can surface at any time, so your fear will forever have power over you and not the other way round. Suppressed fears will often find their expression in some other form that at first may not seem obvious, such as addictive behaviour. On the other hand, if you have the belief that you can defeat fear by boldly facing it head on, then you simply direct it to another part of your mind, rather than healing it. You may appear to have a temporary triumph over your fears, but once again, you are actually giving your fears more power in the long term and becoming more attached to the fear that you are seeking to overcome.

To either avoid the fear or feel the fear is not enough: you need to understand where your fears come from and what they are, freeing the energies that create fear and thus allowing the fears to dissolve into the full embrace of serenity.

FEAR IN THE WORLD

Each of us likes to think that we are independent, but the truth is that our fears link us to one another. We all share, unconsciously, the fears and the experience of fear of every other human being on our small planet.

As we sleep, all human emotion flows through us at a deep level, for sleep is a spiritual device to connect us with one another. Therefore in sleep, alongside love, serenity and the unconscious desire to communicate in a profound non-verbal way, we share our fears.

As we become more consciously aware of our fears, we also begin to heal our fears and those of our fellow human beings while we sleep. In our waking hours we can work out what our own fears are, and in sleep we will experience the underlying serenity in all things.

Fear is the most powerful emotional pollution that affects all people. It encourages the diminishment of women, the abuse of the sacred feminine, poverty, misinformation and the misuse of economics, agriculture and industry. Fear creates environmental pollution, global warming, social unrest, the abuse of human rights, terrorism and global breakdown.

The twentieth century was a time of global fear, as we fought wars on a worldwide scale. Its legacy is potently still with us, but in this new century it is time to let fear go and embrace a new consciousness, allowing last century's fears to fade. The more serenity is brought into the world, the less influential fear will be. However, this requires the courage and maturity of each of us, as we learn to heal our individual fears.

THE JOY OF SERENITY

We are, in our innermost essence, beings of serenity, but we become diverted by fears that lead to confusion and materialism. Serenity, though, is not unreachable. It lies beneath our everyday mind and exists in everyday things. Serenity is the gift that we receive when we are ready to let go of our fears. Fear is simply serenity that has not found itself.

When we find serenity we will learn that it filters out our fears and doubts and embraces the material and spiritual universes, creating a direct experience of the divine in life. Serenity lives within all things and is beyond all religion or philosophy. Serenity is the light of the soul, which reveals the secrets of darkness, fear and shadow that exist within the world and us.

THE WISE AND THE FOOLISH

In each of us there are two parts that fight to make sense of our daily life and all that it throws at us. One part is wise, the other foolish. To find balance in our lives, we need both these parts, for each has a role to play. The suppression of the wise over the foolish, or the foolish over the wise, and the resulting lack of balance, is the source of fear.

If we cling only to the wise, serious and prudent part of ourselves, the foolish part will seek to create havoc, popping up when we are least prepared and prompting us to do things we regret. This foolish part must be acknowledged and accepted, alongside the wise, for the foolish part is also the spontaneous, the free and the joyous part of us.

It is the balance between the wise and the foolish that

makes us human and spiritual and frees us from fear. When the wise and the foolish parts of us are in balance, our lives run smoothly and we are able to take the first step to calm and wellbeing. And as we take this first step, we experience the first flash of serenity.

The Wise Self

Many people feel that wisdom is far removed from their own daily lives and is reserved only for certain special souls who have striven to acquire it through time and great learning. In fact the opposite is true. We all have wisdom, readily accessible, within us and we all use the wise part of ourselves, whether we realise it or not. The wise part of us has deep knowledge and understanding and creates and connects all the undetected structures of our lives merging one to the other, making sense of the unseen. Wisdom brings us the desire for continuity, helps us to understand our fears and prompts us to improve our inner selves and our lives.

The wise part of us also shows us how to be accepting of what we cannot change and to gather courage from all our experiences. The wise self celebrates the hardship of our life's journey, so that we may learn from the lessons that life brings us. It seeks meaning and gathers insights, so that we can unconsciously create fluid yet definable structures in order to make sense of life.

The Foolish Self

Most of us are far more familiar with our foolish selves.

The foolish self can be stupid, silly, brash, self-seeking and unbalanced. It is the part of us that can show off, fool around and indulge in excess. It's easy to be critical of the foolish self. Yet it can also be creative and inspired. The foolish self has ideas and clever impulses and it is full of energy, allowing us to chase our ideals and dreams.

The foolish self seeks serenity but always finds it just out of reach. Yet the foolish self is able to guide us into the mysteries of our inner journey towards freedom from fear and brings us the great lesson that we are not our fears, and that if we are brave, we can overcome these fears. Innocence, love, courage and the opportunity for change are the gifts of the foolish self, which is the catalyst for personal transformation. In embracing the foolish self, we come face to face with the very nature of who we are: our fears, our strengths, weaknesses, wisdom and serenity.

LOSING THE BALANCE

Though each of us is born with the wise and foolish parts of ourself in perfect balance, it easy to lose this relationship. The everyday world encourages us neither to be wise nor foolish but to be second-rate. In this world we are encouraged not to think for ourselves or challenge the way things are but to stay in a state of imbalance, a state in which we remain unhappy, ignorant and fearful. The society we have created, especially in the West, encourages us to be frenetically energetic, over-ambitious and desperately self-aware but not to be courageous or have insight enough to go against the accepted rules. It misunderstands the importance of the foolish part of us while seeking to trivialise the wise part of our being, and does not encourage true life-altering spirituality. When the wise part of us rejects the foolish, it can result in someone who is stiff, guarded and very introverted, finding it difficult to connect with other people. When the foolish attempts to stand alone, rejecting the wise, it results in a person who lives their life in an outward and superficial way, with no inner life or foundation and no ability to use their full potential. While wisdom will seek control and the status quo in order to repress change, the foolish will destroy, break down, rebel and offer no lasting solutions to the needs of people.

BALANCING THE WISE AND FOOLISH SELVES

Each one of us must learn to balance the wise and the foolish in ourself; by learning how to use these qualities, we open ourselves to freedom from fear. This freedom has an almost miraculous quality; it is serene and untroubled, a natural state of consciousness that exists both within the human spirit and within the natural world. With this freedom we are able to be our true selves, at peace no matter what goes on in the world around us.

Although there are similarities and common experiences linking all people in their wisdom and foolishness, the wise and foolish parts within each of us are unique to us and we will each find our own path through the world using our wise aspects and our foolish ones. Therefore to achieve within yourself the balance between these two parts, it is necessary to enter your own internal world.

Learn to hear your own wise and foolish voice and then bring them as one voice out into the world. By listening to your inner guidance and finding the courage to follow its urging, you will be able to create the life that you choose for yourself and to make your life an expression of integrated serenity.

We can only know the wise and foolish when we are brave enough to surrender to them and let go of the fear of self-knowledge. Once we do this, we can use, understand and apply the wise and foolish parts of ourselves in our daily lives. The foolish part can help us deal with all human interaction, guide us to successful communication of our inner needs and help us address issues such as making a living, love and emotional security. The foolish part shows us how to solve our problems without being trapped by them. The wise self comes into play by taking the energy and insight of the foolish self and putting it into a useable structure, thereby giving it meaning and understanding. When the two work together in this way, fear dissolves and serenity becomes fully involved in all your daily thoughts, activities and aspirations.

Let your goal in daily life be to involve yourself in all things with direct and good intention, to let your natural serenity express itself, to enjoy the beauty of life. Always strive for honesty in living what you feel and thereby knowing your own truth.

True serenity comes from understanding the wise and the foolish in yourself and balancing them. Serenity is not static or set in stone but is fluid, dynamic and adaptable.

Meditation to Bring Harmony to the Wise and Foolish Selves

This meditation is simple, profound and inspiring:

Sit in any comfortable position, relaxed and quiet. Close your eyes. Concentrate on the normal cycle of your breathing. In your mind, visualise two balls of light, one white, one blue. The white one is your foolish self, the blue one is your wise self. They orbit around each other slowly in an anti-clockwise motion. Firstly, focus on the blue wise light, allow yourself to merge with it, feel it acting as a channel for all the wisdom, both skilful and unskilful, to flow into you, allow words and images to flow into your body and mind and be absorbed. Now do exactly the same with the white foolish light.

After you have absorbed these two lights, see the same two balls of light shining in your heart, and from these balls within your heart see powerful rays of white and blue light shining out into the world. These lights burn away the dark shadows of your being and permeate everything, awakening your wise and foolish selves and bringing you skilful experiences of life and a deep and abiding serenity.

As you heal the gap between the foolish and the wise within you, and balance them, you will discover the relationship between serenity and fear and free yourself from fear's influence.

David had an extremely stressful job in politics. Day after day he had to make decisions that affected the lives of thousands of people. He felt this to be a huge responsibility and worried endlessly about whether each decision was right. After a while, under the weight of his anxiety and stress, David started to make errors and costly mistakes. As his working life became more troubled and David became more anxious than ever, it affected his relationships with his wife, children and friends. He was irritable, sleepless, depressed, and his health suffered.

A friend of David's recommended that he come to see me. When he arrived, I saw a very troubled man. His shoulders were bowed with the weight he felt he was carrying, he couldn't look me in the eye, and he told me he barely knew how to carry on with his life.

It was very clear that David's wise and foolish selves were seriously out of balance and he was overwhelmed by fear. He was so stiff and guarded that I knew his wise self was rejecting his foolish self and the help and insight it might bring him. He was living his life for outward achievement, with no inner foundation.

I asked David to practise the Meditation to Bring Harmony to the Wise and Foolish Selves. He was unable to see how this might help and was reluctant to try it, but as he was desperate and nothing else had helped, he agreed to go ahead and practise the meditation every day for a month.

When David returned to see me, it was immediately apparent that he was more relaxed. His shoulders were straighter and he looked me in the eye and smiled as he entered my consulting room. He told me that, much to his surprise, the meditation was helping him. He had a strong sense of his wise and foolish selves merging and working together. He felt he was becoming a more cohesive and balanced person and that he was growing in self-knowledge.

David continued with the meditation for a further two months and then practised it at least once a week after that. He was able to reassess his life, make changes and eventually to feel he was back in control, happy in his work and fulfilled in his relationships.

THE TWELVE TYPES OF FEAR

As we attempt to unite and balance our wise and foolish selves, we must also learn to identify the fears that imbalance has created. According to Bön, there are twelve types of fear that dominate our daily lives. We may each of us feel one, several or most of these fears.

Although the root of all fears is that which creates in us attachment, repulsion or powerlessness, individual fears arise from these roots, and these twelve common fears can become part of our emotional reality from our earliest moments in life. The greatest benefit of fear is that when you understand it, you know that you can heal it. It is by identifying the fears we suffer from that we can heal ourselves of them and create a complete and serene life.

These twelve fears are divided into two categories. Firstly, the fears within our daily personality, known as our 'everyday mind', and secondly, the fears that come about in the material world that each of us experiences. The two often mix together, creating a blend of fears that can at first be hard to separate from one another. However, with careful thought and self-examination you can recognise your own particular fears and recognise the extent to which each of them exists within you.

Fears of the Everyday Mind

The fears of the everyday mind are those fears that bring us confusion, pain and suffering and stop us from changing the way we think, feel and act. These fears create the pain of living and the desire for emotional and spiritual change.

1. THE FEAR OF BEING YOURSELF

The fear of being yourself, and of accepting who you are and what you can be, is the foundation of all other fears, for it is to this fear that all fear returns. It is the only fear that all people have, and all eleven other fears emanate from this. The experience of truly knowing yourself is fearful to the everyday mind because it is life-altering. By knowing this fear, understanding it and healing it, we heal all our fears.

2. THE FEAR OF OTHER PEOPLE

The fear of other people is widespread; most people have experienced some fear of another person at some time. This comes about when lack of insight into your own nature creates vulnerability that makes you fear being hurt by others. The fear of other people can be seen globally. It is this fear that causes violence, terrorism, evil and the abandonment of the higher aspects of human nature. And in many societies this fear is encouraged and even glamourised. However, when we give up the fear of others, we discover a profound self-love and a love for life and all living creatures.

3. THE FEAR OF POWER AND CONTROL

There is a belief that having power and control over oneself is the same as having it over others. This is untrue. When you have power and control over yourself, the world will naturally surrender to you, but when you have only external power and control, the world surrenders to your will through coercion, salesmanship, terror, deceit, glamour or seduction. All power and control that is not motivated by inner development, the desire for serenity and the awakening of the best in other people is artificial, and artificial power and control will always become a burden to those who use it. Even power and control over yourself will become an encumbrance if you do not share it with others through acts of love, generosity and concern.

4. THE FEAR OF LOVE

Many people fear love, despite longing for it. The fear of love is the fear of hurt and rejection. When we love, we are exposed and vulnerable; we believe we are at the mercy of those we love. So when you fear love, you fear that if you open up, the other person will discover your shortcomings and reject you. To love is to go behind the shopfront to the storeroom full of insecurities, doubts and longings that we normally keep safely out of sight.

When we love fully, we participate in life utterly and completely. To fear love is to stand back from participating, waiting on the sidelines until it feels safe to step forward. Yet when you find the courage to love fully, you will heal your fear and create a serene inner space where fear cannot go.

5. THE FEAR OF LONELINESS

The fear of loneliness is the fear of loss of intimacy or connection with others and it occurs when we feel that without others we are inadequate and do not fully exist.

If you are afraid of being alone, then you have not discovered the joy of your own company, the pleasure of solitude and the fulfilment that your own internal dialogue can provide.

When you overcome this fear, by embracing the state of aloneness, your life will feel richer. Paradoxically, without the fear of loneliness your contact and communication with others will actually become deeper and more satisfying. People are always drawn to someone who knows themselves and is able to enjoy their own company.

6. THE FEAR OF FEAR ITSELF

For many people their greatest fear is of fear itself. To avoid fear, they hold back from life, becoming isolated and lonely. The fear of fear is a kind of recognition, fear becoming aware of itself, and it is understandable, for it is a recognition of the painful journey fear can take us on.

According to the Tibetan Bön tradition, this fear of fear is not prompted by any outside factor, even if you feel as though it is. It is simply your brain and body teaching itself to become fearful, as it understands the nature of fear. You are fearful because your brain says so, even if there is no cause to be fearful.

7. THE FEAR OF DEATH AND DYING

The fear of death and dying is not fear of the event but of the discovery that comes with death: what will I go through as I die and after my death? This fear is born of the everyday personality that we inhabit for this lifetime. It sees that death will be an end and fears it. But although your personality and form may end at death, the essence of you will not.

The fear of death is a recognition that life is fragile and that nothing lives for ever. What we have to change is the perception that this is a bad thing, for in fact it is not. The experience of death is like a filter that helps to purify our perceptions of death in order that, when we return in another life, each of us may live better lives.

Fears of the Material World

The fears of the material world are those fears that stop us from living successfully and harmoniously in our daily lives. They are the seeds of all material and worldly unhappiness.

8. THE FEAR OF SUCCESS AND FAILURE

The fear of success is identical to the fear of failure. People are fearful of success because it means that not only might their dreams come true but they will have to live out their success and take responsibility for it. It is exactly the same for failure – when we fail we have to accept the loss of dreams and live with our failure, taking responsibility for it. Both are equally hard to deal with; the only difference is that success is more glamorous than failure.

Some people swing from one to the other, finding both equally impossible to accept and live with. Think how many times you have read of a man who becomes a millionaire, loses it all and then makes his fortune all over again, only to lose it once more.

Other people never allow themselves either to succeed or to fail, so great is their fear of both. The only way to overcome this fear is to understand why you need and deserve either your success or your failure. From this understanding comes serenity, which is greater and far more valuable than either success or failure.

9. THE FEAR OF POVERTY AND WEALTH

The fear of either poverty or wealth, of having too much or not enough, is linked, just as the fear of success and failure are linked.

The fear of money and the fear of poverty create anger, for these fears come from the desire to control the material world. Yet when you are in a state of fear, it is virtually impossible to change the material world until the fear is healed. The desire to have lots of money comes from feeling unsafe in the world, while the fear of poverty comes from feeling in constant danger. In our society these fears are denied, as we are constantly encouraged to make money and to see poverty as a personal failing.

To heal the fear of either poverty or wealth, it is important to understand what you have in the world and why and to learn how to use it skillfully. Poverty can be overcome, but if you have the fear of poverty driving you to make money, you will cause great harm to your personality.

10. THE FEAR OF THE FUTURE AND WHAT IT WILL BRING

Most people have moments when they are afraid of what the future will bring. This fear is born of dissatisfaction and the inability to be content with what we have emotionally and spiritually. We feel this fear when we are not fully aware of the value of the life that we have right in front of us, today. We need to take time to consider our current life and situation and to accept it, with all its good and bad aspects. For the emotional and spiritual value in our present life is the catalyst for our connection to serenity, and once we have this connection, we can never again fear the future.

11. THE FEAR OF ACHIEVEMENT AND SELF-ESTEEM

This fear arises when we confuse achievement with a sense of self-esteem and come to believe that they are the same thing. We believe that if we can achieve more, we will raise our self-esteem, but at the same time we fear any achievement, feeling we cannot manage it or cope with it because our self-esteem is low.

The trick here is not to be caught up in this. Achievement of lasting value is the application of your inner knowledge through serenity in the material world. Self-esteem is the benefit that you, and other people, gain from this achievement.

12. THE FEAR OF WAR AND ILLNESS

This fear is a thread running through the history of our species, but today the fear of war is more prevalent than it has ever been. This is because the media has been able to bring war into everyone's living room – something that has never before occurred.

The fear of illness is on the increase too, as we are made aware of the many threats of illness that exist all around us. In the past people lived shorter lives, but they had far fewer fears of illness or war because they were not forced to confront them daily through television, films and newspapers.

We also live in a time of enormous social pressure – to succeed, be wealthy, have certain possessions, live in certain ways and match up to society's expectations. The result is that we live with fear, and in the end fear is the most pervasive and widespread illness of all.

In looking at the lists above, you may have immediately identified with some of them, but this doesn't mean that you don't have any of the others. Most of us have experienced each of these twelve fears in some shape or form at some time. You may also have seen these fears at work in the lives of those around you, your friends, family and colleagues. These fears have a dramatic effect, not just on each individual but on everyone around us and on the world we live in. Take some time to think about yourself and your life. What aspects are you unhappy with and wish to change? What fears lie behind these aspects? Identifying fears in oneself is not always easy. Our deepest fears may not show themselves in any obvious or dramatic way. They are often subtle, pervasive, persuasive, silent and addictive. They support the emotional and spiritual status quo that makes up our daily lives, directing and encouraging many actions and behaviours that we take for granted. Recognising them, and their influence, can be complex and may involve taking a long, hard look at all aspects of our lives.

Fear encourages us to stay stuck and not to embrace change. Therefore an important step towards understanding the fears in your life is to begin with your attitude to change and the unexpected. The more you dislike or avoid change, the greater your underlying fears. If the unexpected alarms or disturbs you, then fear is holding you in its grip.

Once you have identified your fears, you are ready to begin the meditation exercise below. Remember, as you do, that all fear comes to an end and that underneath all of these fears is serenity. When you expose the chattering nature of fear to the clear light of serenity, all fear dissolves.

Meditation on the Twelve Types of Fear

This meditation will safely and peacefully start to loosen all the ties that bind you to each of the Twelve Types of Fear. While practising the meditation, you will gain insights into each of your fears as you experience the serenity that underpins all of them and waits to emerge as a living force in your life.

Begin with the fear that you most strongly identify with, and in time you will be able to work with each of the others. Do not rush; it is important to go forward at a gentle and unhurried pace.

Focusing on the fear that attracts you most, breathe slowly in and out, visualising your breath washing the fear until it is transparent. When this is achieved, see it, in your mind's eye, burst into flames and burn itself out. As it is burning, feel serene energies flow out of your heart into your body, your mind and your daily life.

As you practise this meditation, you will feel a great weight slip from your shoulders. You will become a little larger in thought and deed. Your fear will lose its sting. As you become aware of this, breathe slowly but with intent and see yourself covered in a halo of flames, burning away all your obstructions and revealing innocence and purity.

Remember that in transforming your own fear, you play a part in diminishing the fear in the world. If each one of us learns to live without fear, the world will become serene, free from the painful legacies fear has left.

Despite his rich and varied life and his many material successes, Thomas felt a deep and pervading sense of fear that never left him. He was constantly driving himself on, trying to deal with his fear by making more money and achieving more recognition in the world. But because of his fear, he couldn't enjoy his success – his relationships were troubled and he never felt inner peace.

Thomas came to see me because he felt unwell and depressed. He looked older than his age and appeared care-worn and grey-faced. It soon became clear that he was deeply fearful and regularly experienced all of the Twelve Types of Fear. This stemmed back to a very insecure and bewildering childhood in which he lost his parents and was passed from one foster family to another.

I asked Thomas to try the Meditation on the Twelve Types of Fear, which he agreed to do each day for a month, focusing on one of his fears each time.

When he came back to see me, he looked younger, brighter and healthier. He told me that, as he felt his fears diminish, he was beginning to feel truly alive for the first time in many years.

Six months later, after continuing the meditation daily, Thomas told me he had fallen in love with life. As serenity took the place of the fears in his life, he felt able to partici-pate, where before he had felt like an observer on the side-lines, watching while others lived life to the full. Thomas felt that his life suddenly made sense and he discovered a powerful new sense of direction. Since he had already made enough money, he was able to turn his attention to helping others, and he gained enormous satisfaction from this.

The Serenity Meditation

The Serenity Meditation follows on from the Meditation on the Twelve Types of Fear. Repeat the meditation on the Twelve Types of Fear daily for seven days before moving on to the Serenity Meditation. You can return to the Meditation on the Twelve Types of Fear at any time, but each time you do, repeat it for seven days before performing the Serenity Meditation again.

The Meditation on the Twelve Types of Fear helps you to release and transform your fears. The Serenity Meditation will then enable you to take the next step, which is to discover serenity.

The energy of serenity lies dormant in all things, waiting to be awakened. All that is needed to awaken it in you is your focus and awareness.

Firstly, close your eyes and breathe gently but normally. Then let your mind feel the environment you are in, sensing the space around you. Now send out a request for serenity to flow to you, bringing its blessings to your heart and life. Serenity seeks to bring abundance through wellbeing and happiness, so allow it to come to you. As you start to feel the serenity flow towards you, quietly sing this Bön chant to seal the connection, so that it will not be lost but will grow in quality and strength:

Ah Zha Var Rar
Zha Lha Zha Lha
Var Rar Zha Ah

Sing each word of the chant just as it is written. It is easy, simple and direct. This chant will activate the pathways to serenity that already exist within you and will allow you to forge new and indestructible connections.

Serenity is everlasting and delights in allowing the individual to come alive and into 'being'. Serenity reveals things as they truly are, in their natural and unadorned state. It needs nothing more and is complete in itself and it calls you to experience this sense of completeness for yourself.

In all your daily activities this meditation will show you how to see past the confusion and problems the day may throw at you, to where serenity may be found. In a stressful situation it is easy to lose the connection with yourself. The serenity chant dissolves the stress, releasing the serene energy that is dormant behind it. The chant can also be used to diminish and transform obstacles that keep recurring in your life. The ideal time to do this meditation is first thing in the morning for at least twenty minutes.

Chantal was a young dancer who came to see me after she had been diagnosed with a brain tumour. She was only twenty-two and had been living a life that was active, fun and exciting. When she began to experience intermittent blindness and numbness, she ignored it, until at last her worsening symptoms forced her to see a doctor. The diagnosis was devastating. Chantal had a brain tumour that was inoperable and growing rapidly. She did not have long to live.

She came to see me in a state of panic and fear. I encouraged her to practise the Meditation on the Twelve Types of Fear, focusing on the fear of death, daily for a week and to follow this with the Serenity Meditation. I suggested that she then continue to practise both meditations twice a day.

Over the next few months these meditations helped Chantal to calm her fears and face her illness with serenity. Her true friends drew close to her, and she came to understand that even though her body was sick, she was whole and well inside.

When Chantal died, her serene state was so powerful that it healed her family's devastation at losing their only child at such a young age. Chantal discovered the true nature of inner calm and wellbeing, and through her example so did others.

2

BEING YOURSELF

Being yourself is the height of all achievement and what all people ultimately want. To be yourself, without pretence of any kind, without the need for putting up a defensive front, without fear of judgement by others, is the foundation for all true inner discovery and spiritual exploration.

Being yourself begins with acceptance of all that you are, have been and will be. When you cannot be yourself, it is because you are afraid, so the path to acceptance and to being yourself begins with the release of fear. When you have transformed your fear into serenity and are truly able to be yourself, you will be ready to take the further path, from being to becoming, from acceptance of who you are now, to the fulfilment of all that you may become.

The power of fear creates the desire to cling to the fear itself. To overcome fear, you need to move from the fears shared by the crowd to the fearless freedom of the individual that you are. This takes courage. As you do this, you will start to become yourself and fear will lose its grip. In this state of courageous individuality you can then awaken the spiritual forces of change. This can be done through growing up, work, career, having a family, intellectual training, emotional development or spiritual awakening as well as through the experience of profound love.

In the last chapter we looked at the importance of balancing the wise and the foolish parts of yourself and of identifying which of the Twelve Types of Fear affects you the most deeply. In this chapter we will go on to find out more about when and how your fears have developed and how they affect you on a daily basis, keeping you from being yourself. We will also look at the Seven Ages of Fear – the stages of life in which different fears can develop – so that you can begin to understand when certain fears arose in your own life. Finally, we will look at happiness – what it is, how important it is, why so many people pursue it and the source of true happiness, which is knowing your own heart.

KEEPING A JOURNAL

To begin to understand how fear affects you day by day, start keeping a journal. The purpose of the journal is to look at the ebb and flow of your fears. It is not for losing yourself in your fears but rather for standing back and watching what comes and goes. This way you learn to know the types of fear you have, the cycles of your fears and how they stop you from being yourself.

Start your journal on any weekday and note down each time you feel a fear, small or large, and in what context – for instance, is it in certain situations?, does it involve other people?, or is it internal and unconnected to external events? Keep your journal daily for a month without going back through it or analysing it. After a month find a quiet and reflective time to read it all the way through. What information emerges? Perhaps the same pattern of fear repeats itself regularly. Perhaps fears have appeared that you were unaware of. Perhaps you can see the ways in which you sabotage or undermine yourself through fear.

Through your journal you can discover how you allow fear,

in any of its forms, to stop you being yourself. As you see the patterns emerge and the themes of fear in your daily life, you will begin to identify the impulses behind your fears. This will be a huge step towards changing those impulses and releasing your fears.

When you have examined your journal in depth and distilled its essence, then, quietly and with reverence, burn it, seeing the flames purifying and transforming this collection of fearful patterns.

THE SEVEN AGES OF FEAR

The fear of being yourself often starts very young and, unless you halt it and begin to transform and release your fears, gradually grows in influence until your death. To understand this aspect of fear, which is of paramount importance, you need to examine the experiences of fear that you have had at different stages of your life.

Tibetan Bön breaks down these experiences into the Seven Ages of Fear. Bön teachings do not talk of fault or sin or blame but regard the fears we develop as a means of dealing with the unknown and the force of ignorance.

What follows is an outline of each of the Seven Ages of Fear, with a specific meditation for each intended to dissolve the fears developed at that particular age. But first I will give you a powerful, safe and helpful meditation to be used as the basis for each of the individual meditations for the Seven Ages of Fear.

Meditation on the Seven Ages of Fear

When using this meditation, begin by focusing on the age

you are at present. After that you can meditate on your past ages, particularly those when life-changing events occurred or when you were unhappy. It is also possible to meditate on your future ages and the hopes you have for them.

Sit comfortably. Close your eyes. Breathe in and out slowly and normally, concentrating on the movement of your breath throughout your body. Let your mind rest in the action of your breathing for several minutes.

Now, think of your body starting to shrink, slowly becoming smaller and smaller until all that you feel is your heartbeat. At this point let your concentration merge with the age you are working with.

This meditation will not only reveal your fear, what it means and its influence on you, it will also reveal your levels of serenity, contentment and wellbeing, for as you have fear, so you have an equal measure of serenity.

1. CONCEPTION TO BIRTH

Even before birth a child in the mother's womb can see, feel, hear, touch and taste. According to ancient Tibetan belief, the child is also able to reason, consciously and unconsciously, at twenty-eight weeks after conception and is profoundly influenced by all that enters into its world – the world of the mother's womb. The worries of the child's parents, in particular those of the mother, are conveyed to the child and can become the future underlying fears of the child's personality. To understand this, look at what you consider your most powerful fear, the fear that stops you from being yourself. This will almost always be a fear that developed in the womb and will be connected to what was going on at the time in the lives of your parents.

The fears that develop at this age are those of confusion and the inability to focus and concentrate, as well as the fear of not being able to trust other people and the fear of the unknown.

MEDITATION ON LIFE IN YOUR MOTHER'S WOMB

After meditating as described in the general meditation on page 31, you are ready for the next step.

At this point begin to see yourself forming as a foetus. Let the time in the womb between this moment of forming and your birth flow gently past you, scene by scene, only stopping when a fear presents itself. If this happens, stop, name the fear aloud and write down the fear and how you felt in that moment. This is all you need to do. This meditation can be repeated as often as you wish.

---

2. BIRTH TO SEVEN YEARS

At this point in a child's life, they are coming to terms with the delights and restrictions of the five senses and the power of the emotions. It is in this time that a child becomes aware of the bigger world outside themself. During these years a child will start to be aware of the impermanence of all things and of pain and death. In addition, the child will learn that life changes and that they cannot have things all their own way. It is also a time in which intellectual potential develops, alongside an awareness of happiness and unhappiness. It is a time when the spiritual and material begin to make themselves felt. The fears that develop at this age are loneliness, powerlessness, inferiority, insecurity, a feeling of worthlessness and a fear of intimacy.

MEDITATION ON THE YEARS BETWEEN BIRTH AND SEVEN

Having begun with the general meditation, focus on the years from birth until seven, seeing yourself as a newborn infant, then a toddler and then a young child. Let every year flow past your mental vision; once again any important fear or situation that created fear within you will naturally present itself to you. When the fear appears, stop meditating, name it aloud and then write it down.

3. SEVEN TO FOURTEEN YEARS

This is the period of time in which the emotions and the body start to work together. It is in these years that the emotional, spiritual, physical and intellectual potentials start to become integrated within the individual, establishing personality and habits.

The child's mind starts to become more rational and search for the meaning behind events in their own life as well as in the world. It is in this time, regardless of gender, that the great feminine forces of the natural world stir in the child and emerging young person, like the crocus flower that blooms through a layer of snow. Awakening and awareness are the themes of this age.

The fears that develop at this time are insecurity, fear of the physical world and of one's body, awareness of unfulfilled potential and poor communication. Fear of or addiction to sexual impulses and behaviour can also develop at this point. It is in this age that our fears become powerfully etched into the behavioural patterns that will guide us in later life.

MEDITATION ON THE YEARS BETWEEN SEVEN AND FOURTEEN

After beginning with the general meditation, allow these years to pass through your mind's eye, one by one. Connect with the dreams you had in these years. Remember the poetry in your soul that was emerging, the wonder of learning and the realisation that life could be of your own making. Reflect also upon the first understandings of how the world around you tried to stop you from being yourself. See your fears dissolving and return to the sense of being yourself which was yours before fears took over.

4. FOURTEEN TO TWENTY-ONE YEARS

In these years the power and challenges of the young person's individuality begin to be put to the test and the adult that they will become emerges. It is in these years that fears begin to limit the young person and can obstruct them from having the life they want. It is in these years that they learn to be afraid and gain a rational awareness of their fears. This is the time when the emerging adult can learn to be afraid and not to love to their full potential. These years are crucial, for they can lead to the young person closing down or prompt them to move beyond their family and upbringing to lead a life that reflects their inner potential. The particular fears that can arise at this time relate to identity and responsibility for the self, for at this stage adult behaviour is being formed.

MEDITATION ON THE YEARS BETWEEN FOURTEEN AND TWENTY-ONE

Begin with the general meditation and then focus upon your heart, feeling its beat and connecting with its rhythm. Allow forgiveness and a sense of openness and exploration to dwell in your heart. Let the memories return and discover, hidden in your heart, the truths of your being. If you are in this age group, allow the qualities of these years to open new pathways of growth for you. Do not be afraid. Let your fears dissolve into yourself so that you can be yourself.

5. TWENTY-ONE TO THIRTY-ONE YEARS

These are the years of knowing how to act in the world. During this time life either becomes a friend or a series of obstacles, and the knocks that life gives you become a catalyst for change or a perpetual reference to resentment and hurt. Unskilful thinking at this time limits attitudes and opportunities, for this is the time when most people start to grow up. In the Bön tradition people only really come of age when they reach twenty-seven, for this is when the spirit, body and mind learn to cooperate. It is when we discover the art of becoming mature and learn the lasting lessons of partnership, relationships and the love that we need to give in order to gain from our human experience. Here the strongest underlying fear is of impermanence. This can lead to inner panic and a feeling that there is not enough time in life to do everything. It is also common, at this stage, to develop the fear of leaving youth behind and being alone in the world.

MEDITATION ON THE YEARS BETWEEN TWENTY-ONE AND THIRTY-ONE

After the general meditation, feel your heartbeat and let the experiences you have had in this period flow unhindered into your heart. Recognise the fears you have felt during this time and sense yourself learning and growing through them. It is time to understand what you have experienced and to let go, seeing your fears dissolve within you and emerging strong, clear and serene.

6. THIRTY-ONE TO SIXTY-ONE YEARS

This time is about the expression of what the adult knows and the discovery of what he or she does not know. It is the time to seek the truths in life and to grow up, making, creating and returning resources and experiences to the family and larger community. It is also a time to gather wisdom, yet this is often the time when we allow fears to affect us the most and the unresolved fears from our past become the events of our present experience.

It is at this stage in life that we can learn the most about the impermanence of all that we hold to be important, and if we cannot accept this impermanence, it can lead to a great fear of loss and of death.

MEDITATION ON THE YEARS BETWEEN THIRTY-ONE AND SIXTY-ONE

Acceptance of the past and what it can teach you is the theme in this part of the meditation. Begin with the general meditation and then focus upon your heart. Become aware of the nature of your fear and how it has contributed to your life's path. Now dissolve these fears into your heart, feel the acceptance that comes from this meditation, and embrace it.

---

7. SIXTY-ONE YEARS TO DEATH

In the West these are sometimes termed the 'twilight years'. This is ridiculous, for it is the newly born who are in the twilight as they descend from out of a vaster awareness into a confused and mixed sensory experience. For the older person, this period is one of awakening, transcendence and power. Whether their fear has increased or decreased, whether they are comfortable with who they are or not, this is not a time of resignation but a time of action through contemplation, sharing and knowing one's own value.

For those who are afraid of being themselves, this is the perfect time to overcome this, for then death will be a simpler and more joyous affair. Death is a personal experience, which each one of us must go through alone, and our state of fear, serenity and acceptance will have a marked impact on the way we die. Our unresolved fears accompany us through our dying and death, so it is greatly preferable to transform our fears before death.

MEDITATION ON THE YEARS BETWEEN SIXTY-ONE AND DEATH

Begin with the general meditation and then become aware of your heart beating. It could stop at any moment, yet each beat is a call to wake up and to the mystery behind all life and the role your life has within the greater scheme of things. Let go of your fears now and see them dissolving inside you. You have the great adventure ahead of you – the first glimpse of the clear light of eternity – so gather your power to you in readiness. Let all of your power dissolve now into your heart and there you will find the beat of life.

Darla was a young woman who came to see me in great distress. She had a very successful career in showbusiness and was a household name, her face instantly recognisable, yet she was consumed by fear. Her celebrity and fortune had only increased her fear of losing everything and being left penniless and alone.

It soon emerged, as we talked, that at the age of ten Darla had lost her mother in a car accident and her life had changed overnight. Left in the care of relatives by her father, who felt unable to cope, the whole foundation of her world had crumbled, leaving her desperately insecure and feeling abandoned.

I taught Darla the Meditation on the Years Between Seven and Fourteen and suggested she repeat it daily for twenty minutes for three months.

When Darla came back, she looked very different. Softer and more open, she smiled more and spoke with more confidence. She told me that as she had meditated on her fear of loss and abandonment, she had understood why she was so afraid to be herself. She understood that her efforts to avoid being herself had led to the creation of her showbiz persona, a glamorous façade to hide behind so that no one would see the real her.

Darla's transformation had begun. Over the next few months she became calmer and more confident. She made the decision to take time out from her showbiz career to spend with the people she loved and to work with young children who had been bereaved as she once had.

Today Darla feels safe in the world in a way that she hadn't since before her mother's death. She is a whole, rounded and very warm person, fully in charge of her life and happy to be herself.

Harry was a man of sixty-nine who came to see me after his only daughter, who was in her thirties, had been killed in a hit-and-run accident. Harry's wife had died of cancer some years before.

The death of his daughter had broken Harry's spirit. He felt fearful of being alone, fearful of living and of dying and so distraught that he had become trapped in his own fearful response to the tragedy in his life.

I treated Harry for his distress and asked him to begin the Meditation on the Years Between Sixty-one and Death.

At the same time I encouraged him to ask for support from friends and family and to talk to a bereavement counsellor.

Bravely, Harry did all of these things and gradually he found some peace of mind. As his fear of death – his own as well as those he loved – diminished, he was able to feel more positive about life.

A year after his loss Harry felt well enough to go out with friends and to plan a trip abroad. While his grieving would undoubtedly go on, he was able to live his life with optimism and tranquillity and without feeling crushed by what had happened to him.

FEAR IN MEN AND WOMEN

At this point it is important to recognise that, when it comes to fear, there is a difference between the sexes, both in the way fear is felt and in the way it is expressed.

Bön teachings say that men express fear non-verbally through their bodies and are stimulated to actively try to contain the fear. Women, however, express fear throughout their entire being, allowing it to pass through them. It is these different ways of experiencing fear that lead to misunderstanding and conflict between the sexes. The powerful forces of fear create unseen confusion between men and women. Intangible fears influence both men and women equally, but men express intangible fear indirectly, while women will experience a direct physical manifestation of it, passing it into the material world through a thought, action, idea, event or object.

This is why, according to Bön teachings, it is best to follow the feminine expression of fear and, by manifesting it, change it. This process takes its power away and turns the latent power inherent in fear into understanding. So whether male or female, to overcome the fear of being yourself, it is important to know how aligned you are to the feminine forces of the natural world that live within you, for this is the healing force of this type of fear.

KNOWING YOUR OWN HEART

The key to truly being yourself is knowing your own heart and following it. Have you ever experienced a moment or situation when other people did not want you to follow your heart? When you were stopped from expressing what you really felt or from following a course of action you felt strongly drawn to? If so, take time to consider how that made you feel.

Though those who held you back may have had the best of intentions, they stopped you from following your heart and thus from being yourself, and that is often a painful experience. When we are prevented from following our hearts and being ourselves, we shrink, learning to hold back and not to trust our own judgement. When we are encouraged to be ourselves, we grow in wisdom, understanding and joy.

The experience of following your heart is powerful and dynamic and moves you beyond your old boundaries of experience. When you know how to read your own heart, you naturally acquire understanding of the hearts of others, for all hearts are linked and beat the same beat. So to follow your own heart is also to grow in wisdom, compassion and generosity towards others.

Knowing your heart is knowing what makes you who you are. It is knowing your reason for wanting life. One of the ways to know your own heart is to be in nature and to see it, not with your eyes, but with the understanding in your heart. Your heart then becomes your true eye on the world.

It is not always easy in today's world to know or follow your own heart. There are many people who know in their hearts what is right but who hesitate to follow what they know, waiting for others to act first and take the lead. In this way each person waits for the other and the only thing that happens is waiting. So be brave, follow your heart, even when that means standing up to be counted. You will know yourself best when your heart is inspired by ideals and beliefs that bring you serenity and simplicity. And the more truly you follow your heart and know yourself, the more others will see beauty in you and be drawn to you. Live your life with compassion and love for others, guided by the pure, clear voice of your heart, and your spirit will grow. And as it does, you will move from just being – when you are purely reactive – to becoming – when all life is with you and in you. You will move from going with the flow to becoming part of the flow of life.

THE PURSUIT OF HAPPINESS

The idea that we want or deserve happiness or that we should actively pursue it is a very recent one. Until recently people's lives revolved around survival. They were far too busy trying to meet their basic needs for food and warmth to have time to think about happiness.

Today in much of the world people experience peace, live longer, healthier lives, and enjoy improved human rights and individual freedom, all part of an increase in prosperity in the last 120 years.

For many of us, especially in the West, our basic needs are now met with very little effort and so we have the luxury of time to contemplate other things we might like or want. It is natural to human beings to pursue status and we have developed a culture of 'more', where we seek after more material wealth, more security and more happiness.

The irony is that, despite this, people are less happy and more fearful today than they were fifty years ago. In the past people simply didn't think about being happy, whereas we are now largely unhappy, because with the status we have pursued comes a new level of anxiety. We have less need to worry than ever and yet we worry more.

The more we acquire and long for goods and possessions, the more fearful we become of being without them and the less we are able to focus on spiritual growth. And the less we focus on spiritual growth, the more we separate from our inner selves and the more fearful we feel.

Alongside material wealth we expect happiness as our right and want it to be instant. Today in rich Western nations more food is produced than can be consumed, every little luxury is regarded as a necessity, and people are bombarded with goods and services. This creates discontent, and so we seek 'happiness' as an antidote.

We look for things to make us 'happy' – a holiday, a car, a house, a new relationship – and instantly change things that we consider make us 'unhappy', whether that is a husband or wife or a piece of clothing. We clamour for whatever we have decided we want; we envy those who seem to have it. We think that if we get richer, thinner, divorced, younger, more spontaneous, fitter, married, pregnant or promoted, we'll be happy. But all that happens is we get caught up in our problems.

As more and more people distance themselves from their spiritual nature with a carpet of comfort, the fear of living takes on an even greater power. People find it harder to spend time in their own company and seek lesser substitutes for serenity through consumerism and gratification of the senses. Consumerism and sensual gratification have their place – all people have searched for these since the beginning of civilisation – but in today's 'instant' world each of us needs to be more careful in our choices and discriminating in our actions. Today we know less about our world, our local communities, our ways of living and human relationships than our great-grandparents and our grandparents did, and it is easier to lose ourselves than it has ever been.

A chasm has appeared between the promise and the delivery of the material world. As the world becomes richer, people are becoming less happy and are experiencing increasing levels of fear. This is because as more people become dissatisfied and search for quick fixes, they are unwittingly broadcasting their fear to an already fragile world – a fear born out of separation from our inner nature and the natural world.

However, changes are beginning to happen. As unhappiness increases, so does the fear that causes the unhappiness. Gradually, material goods and power are losing their appeal, as we realise they are not the answer, and many people are now seeking lifestyle changes and looking for a way to live wisely. People across the world are searching for meaning in their lives and beginning to take a spiritual path. Our world is in transition from the need to survive to the need to make sense of the world around us and to find fulfilment.

FINDING HAPPINESS

Happiness in the everyday world rises like swells of waves upon the sea, changing, subsiding, reforming and never lasting. Within us, however, happiness is born from the clear light of consciousness. Yet we are often strangers to ourselves in the search for happiness, unaware that inside us are the answers to all our questions.

According to Bön teachings, you can learn how to be happy and stay happy. When fear is healed, happiness will be present, because as you achieve serenity you will also achieve happiness. And when you heal fear, you recognise that happiness is not somewhere else but in the place that you are, and not for another day but for this day. All you have to do is invite it into your heart.

Happiness achieved in this way is lasting. It is present whether you have a good day or a bad one, whether things go right or wrong. It is a part of you, there with you whatever is going on around you, dependent only on you and not on circumstances.

Happiness is not an unattainable luxury. It is your natural-born right to be happy. The Bön teachers have taught for thousands of years that by transforming body and mind, happiness is released from our inner resources. According to Tibetan wisdom, you can change your brain and central nervous system to safely release the inner happiness that is waiting to be discovered. It is stored in us as energy. Now, recent scientific developments in neurology – the study of the brain and nervous system – are confirming this and showing that happiness can be registered by changes in the brain and is real and easily accessible. If you are unhappy then you suffer. Your health, energy, work and relationships will all worsen. So to achieve happiness is a form of wisdom – the wisdom of skilful and non-aggressive survival.

Those who understand true happiness know that you do not have to focus directly upon your problems to fix them; instead, you must find all the possibilities of change within them and then turn those possibilities into reality. Simply doing this will create happiness.

Another avenue of happiness is to connect with other people at a straightforward level by talking, sharing activities and playing a part in your community. In the same way, our inner wellbeing depends on simple things, not complicated ones: exercise, sleep, having close relationships, enjoying friendships, developing an optimistic outlook on your life and acknowledging your emotions. Forgiveness and fraternity create happiness. The increase in unhappiness in Western society, characterised by chronic stress, discontent and boredom, is creating a spiritual auto-immune disease, which is eating away individual and social integrity.

It is more important to have happiness here and now than to try to make a big, complicated plan to be happy at some point in the future. Happiness doesn't work that way. Happiness is the thread that links your life, moment to moment. The more you try to make happiness last, the less likely it will be to happen. If you can learn to simply enjoy a moment of happiness, then it will become part of this thread and it will last.

Bring happiness into your life by sharing it. Talk about being happy, think about making others happy and happiness will turn up of its own accord in your life. And as you increase happiness, you decrease fear and allow serenity into your life.

Happiness is ultimately a personal choice. It depends on how we are prepared to see the world and our role in it. Do you have the courage to go beyond your fears and embrace the change within to release your happiness potential? Happiness is indestructible. Like serenity, it is inside us, waiting to be released. It is not dependent on any material or circumstantial change in your life but rather on your own willingness to welcome it into your life.

Meditation to Create Happiness

Meditation is not something you do but rather it is the discovery and release of a natural state of consciousness and the expression of this state. This meditation will allow you to release the happiness within you and create the right expression for it, so that it constantly creates and recreates itself in your life.

Sitting comfortably, let your eyes close. Focus on your breathing; let it be natural and not forced. As you become aware of your breathing, imagine that your breath is creating a shining tube from your nose down into the centre of your physical heart. As you breathe, your heart pulses and bright blue energy flows up from it, mingling with your incoming and outgoing breath. As you do this, see yourself becoming surrounded by a bright blue mist of energy that is absorbed into your skin and body. You feel the blue mist permeating throughout you. As this happens, the first great wave of happiness flows out of your heart, encompassing you. You are immersed in happiness. The blue mist now flows as a great torrent out of your heart into your breath, and an endless and continual cascade flows over you. Let yourself be immersed in it.

Michael and Sherry were a couple who didn't know how to be happy. They had been married for fifteen years and most of that time they had been miserable together. Yet they told me that they could not bear to be apart. Everything else in their lives ran smoothly; they had no material problems and no obvious reasons for their unhappiness other than an unformed sense of discontent with one another. They had got into the habit of arguing, putting one another down and sulking.

I asked them both to do the Meditation to Create Happiness, separately, for a month. During this time they were not to discuss it with one another but were simply to practise the meditation and observe their own reactions. I asked them also, during this time, to make an agreement to treat one another with respect and kindness. At times when they felt they could not do this, I asked them to walk away, rather than argue.

After a month they came to see me to report on their progress. Both felt calmer, more joyful and more positive about the marriage. After two further months of practising both the meditation and their new behaviours towards one another, they reported that they both felt a big shift in their relationship.

What Michael and Sherry learnt is that unhappiness can become a habit, which, like any other, is hard to break. Only effort and regular focusing on happiness and kind behaviour will turn habitual unhappiness around.

3

OTHER PEOPLE

Other people are our greatest challenge in life, for we are so deeply linked to others that we *are* one another. Other people are simply ourselves in another guise, and we unconsciously seek ourselves in others. We search in the actions of others for meaning in our own lives, and it is by the thoughts and actions of others that we gain understanding, love, power, mercy, fear, freedom and serenity.

If we could see what we have in common with other people, we would know that countless opportunities for serenity and fearless living take place every day in our exchanges with them, no matter how brief these exchanges might be. Yet all too often we miss these opportunities because, rather than seeing what we have in common, we see only what divides us and the result is fear, mistrust and hostility.

Understanding our connections with other people is vital if we are to find serenity in our lives. In this chapter I will explain how each one of us is connected to every person on this planet and how we can learn about ourselves through the way we observe and understand the thoughts and actions of other people. When we understand the powerful connection between ourselves and others, we find the meaning we have been seeking. Other people are our spiritual teachers and, if we are willing, they can show us the path to growth, understanding and freedom from fear.

The people who are present in our daily lives represent the

connections that we most need to understand. This includes people in all areas of life – work, friends, family, neighbours and others in our local community. These people we see every day or live with are the gateways to greater understanding. It is important to embrace them in our thoughts with respect and joy, knowing that through our relationship with them we will learn and grow, spiritually and emotionally. Extending respect and kindness is not always easy, particularly in connections with others that we find challenging or difficult. However, it is often in these very connections that our greatest opportunities for learning lie. Every human being is a miracle, yet all too often fear would have us not believe in the miraculous.

In the Bön tradition the connections we make with others, and thus of course with ourselves, are encapsulated in what is called the Eleven Paths of Human Experience. These eleven paths are meditations on human nature and are used to gain insight into ourselves and other people.

Later in this chapter we will explore each of the eleven paths in detail. For the moment, however, I would like you to look carefully and slowly through the list of the paths and have a sense of how, in each of these areas, other people have affected you most profoundly. Let each one stir memories of experiences, hopes, aspirations, achievements, failures, losses and loves.

1. Work
2. Love, mercy and grace
3. Anger and anxiety
4. Illness
5. Family
6. Friendship
7. Self-esteem

8. Integrity
9. Forgiveness
10. Spiritual development
11. Daily living

FEARFUL CONNECTIONS

All too often we look not at what we have in common with others but at our differences. Instead of looking for links, we look for divisions. Instead of approaching one another with love, we approach with mistrust, hostility or doubt. This is because underlying everything else is fear, and we seek out the unskilful and negative to reinforce this fear. Fear keeps us bound to material events and habits, and the result of this is anxiety. Anxiety is the acceptable face of fear; we talk of being anxious when actually we are simply fearful. Anxiety is more prevalent now than at any other time in history. We live in anxious times, which means that fear is becoming a normal part of life for many people. We expect to be fearful and we are forgetting how not to be. Serenity and integration are seen to be too much hard work.

Becoming wealthier and having more possessions is actu-ally making us more anxious. And many people, in their fearful and anxious states, look for solutions to heal their fear. Rather than accepting fear, with its gifts of great energy and heightened awareness, and then transforming it into serenity, they try to fight it. As people seek solutions to the problems of living, born of the rift between the wise and foolish impulses, instant solutions have become hugely popular in today's world. Some people choose to fight fear with instant spirituality, in which glamour parades as wisdom and passivity as serenity. Instant spirituality is a modern creation, first formed in the new age of the late twentieth century. It seeks to help people with their emotions but in reality only gratifies insecurity and neediness. Although it provides a kind of comfort blanket to the believer, instant spirituality cannot do anything about fear, for it is a form of fear itself. Spirituality has become both fashionable and necessary, as people realise that there is a gap in their lives. Spirituality and emotional wellbeing are now as important in the popular imagination as the latest trend in fashion, advice on careers or relationships. Yet if they are viewed in this way, fear overtakes them and spirituality becomes neurosis and anxiety. To genuinely move forward, fear must be healed and serenity activated. And fear is healed through living in the real world in daily life and finding serenity in the essence of the ordinary. It takes its own time.

One of the prime ways to resolve anxiety, and thus fear, is not to own more, earn more, find material 'security' or turn to instant spirituality but to make connections with others that feed us, enrich us and teach us.

Fear can be transformed through friendship. A true friend is the one who, rather than proffering advice, solutions or cures, is willing to share our pain and our wounds. The friend who can be silent with us in despair or confusion, who stays with us through grief and bereavement, who can tolerate not knowing the solution and simply be there for us is a gift in the form of another person. Through such friendships we have the opportunity to gain insight, heal our fears and have a direct experience of serenity.

Just as a person can be transformed by the power of another's belief in them, so fear can be transformed into serenity through the power of positive belief. Indeed, constant belief in the goodness of others is the transmission of fear into serenity. And in the face of serenity fear loses its power and evolves into knowledge, love and understanding.

ILLNESS AND DEATH

Illness is a time when we are in especial need of other people. We become fearful of serious illness because it forces us to recognise that we are powerless. We must accept the fact that we are ill. The only choice we have is to accept the illness and decide to heal or give in to the fear of the unknown and die. And whichever choice we make we need other people, to help us to heal and live, or to die.

The seeds of health are in every illness and these seeds are fear and serenity. They offer us information not only on illness and health but also on life and what life really is. When other people are ill, seriously or otherwise, what is your reaction? When you react to the illness of others, you are reacting to the very same illness within yourself. Our reaction to illness tells us how much we identify with the illness and how much it scares us. Illness reminds us that we are fragile and easily destroyed.

Illness is information, so our fears about illness and health become a warehouse of self-knowledge if we are willing to explore them. At their essence is serenity, and if we are willing to accept the illness and to learn from it, our fears will dissolve and we will experience the serenity that may lead us back to health.

Serenity also transforms the experience of death. If you live life based upon your connection to serenity, rather than thinking that death is an ending or something to fear, illness and even death become simply an opportunity to pause for reflection.

My teacher sat by the fire. The Pururi trees stood around us, some gnarled and twisted, others straight and dark in the dappled light. The forest was silent in the way that all deep forest in New Zealand is – not an absence of noise but a doorway to serenity. We had just finished a lesson on how all things are connected.

I held a spoon in my hand. 'So, Ürgyen, this spoon is connected to all other spoons in the world?' I asked.

'No,' he said. 'Not by itself but through the idea that the spoon does what it does. This connects it and makes it at the same time very special and very ordinary. So it is with people. A spoon is happy doing what it does best, and so it is for people; they are happy doing what they do best.'

'Is that a job or a belief?' I asked.

'Neither,' he said. 'It is when they become human and then they discover that is what they are meant to be doing. Just being human. It doesn't need a belief; it is itself, naturally imbued with serenity.'

The little stream that hurried past us suddenly sounded deafening, as did the tall Pururi trees growing straight up towards the sky. His words hung in the air.

ALLOWING OURSELVES TO BE HUMAN

The above lesson on the importance of allowing ourselves our humanity has stayed with me. The route to serenity begins by allowing ourselves to be human and we do this by allowing ourselves to dissolve our isolation and loneliness into shared experience with other people. In this way we begin to heal our fear.

Our first step is to enjoy other people for who they are and to recognise that serenity flows directly to us through the person with whom we are interacting. Our enjoyment then becomes love for our fellow human beings, a powerful force that binds each person to the other.

We forget the power contained in the word 'life'. Each of our lives is filled with glory. We have the ability to live in glory every day that we take part in life. We must not forget it and allow ourselves to be dominated by habit and emotional confusion or forgetfulness – all the trappings of fear.

Have you ever walked down the street and seen each person that you pass as a friend? Have you seen what another person felt as you passed them, or sensed what they experience? Fear demands that you do not. Serenity states that you can. If you see the world as a place full of friends, then no town is unknown, no person need be a stranger. If you start to heal your own fear by extending friendship, you will help to heal the fears of others. As you experience serenity, so will other people.

Simply by existing, our fellow human beings provide us with opportunities for giving and receiving love in all kinds of ways, from the unexpected kindness of strangers to the love of a special person.

AWAKENING SERENITY

All our lessons in life come to us through the thoughts, actions and deeds of others. And to experience love and compassion with others, all we need is serenity.

The following invocation will allow you to awaken the serenity waiting inside you. Sit quietly in a peaceful space and recite it aloud. As you do, try to recall the memories that you evoked when you thought about each of the Eleven Paths of Human Experience. As you speak the lines of the invocation, it will awaken, then reveal all of your own experiences of the Eleven Paths of Human Experience, dissolve your fear and bring to you a direct experience of serenity.

Listen to yourself as you speak each line. Pause between lines to breathe in and out. Consider the importance of each line and say each line with focus and direct intent. Not only are you affirming these lines within you, you are directing them with your mental force and consciousness to become real in the everyday world. In using this, you gain direct experience of what all of us have in the end to face: becoming our own truth, the truth of the human experience, which flows unhindered through all people.

An Invocation to Awaken Serenity: A Daily Reminder for Self-knowledge

Essentially, it is not important what I do for a living
I must know what my heart aches for
Do I dare to dream of facing my heart's longing?
It is not important how old I am
It is important that I am prepared to look like a fool
For my dreams and beliefs,
For love
And for the great adventure of being alive.

It is not important what astrological sign I was born under
But it is important that I know
The spiritual and emotional depths of my being.

It is important for me to know
If life's hardships have dried out my heart and
If I believe that I cannot feel anything any more.

Can I sit with pain, others' or my own, without seeking to hide it, fix it or
     change it?
Can I live with joy, my own or others'?
Can I live with spiritual wildness?
And let ecstasy fill all of me
And go on beyond the accepted limitations of what it is to be human?

Can I be true to myself regardless of what it may cost me in family,
     friends, wealth or reputation?
Can I find the courage not to betray my soul?

Can I be faithful and trustworthy to myself?
Can I see beauty when ugliness surrounds me?
Can I live with failure, mine and other people's?

It is not important in the larger story of my life
Whether I have material wealth, status or success
What is important is if I can get up
After hardship or a restless night,
Face the day and do what is right and true
Can I stand in my own light and not shrink back from its brilliance?

I know that what sustains me, when all else fails, is the inner serenity
     that lives within me.
I can be alone with myself and like my own company
In the quiet moments of my life
Its meaning will be clear.

I can give myself the gift of self-knowledge, serenity and freedom from fear.

THE ELEVEN PATHS OF HUMAN EXPERIENCE

So now let us explore the Eleven Paths of Human Experience. In each of them you will find effective ways to understand people better and to have peaceful relations with everyone you meet, so that ultimately you will find fear no longer has a place in your experience of other people.

Each path will help you to gain the understanding with which to overcome fear and increase your serenity. Each of them will pose questions and give you the chance to find answers, and each will be a guide to understanding an aspect of other people. Treat these paths as a journey of meditation and contemplation, moving you towards a deeper knowledge of other people's fears and serenity, as well as your own.

These paths are directed to your soul through the medium of words. Use your mind to understand them but be aware that it is your soul that will act upon them. Take your time and consider their place in your life. Through this study of the energy of other people, you will find out who you are, have been and shall become. You will also learn what you are not.

Let us now begin to explore each of these eleven paths.

1. WORK

Work is not merely an activity; it is an interaction created by and with other people. When we work, we are making relationships. Any problems that we have at work come from the way we deal with others and their fears – and no matter how large or small your workplace, others you work with or for share the same fears and the same potential for serenity.

Therefore, in order to understand yourself better at work, you need to understand the other people you work with – what are their fears?, and what do they want from life? This doesn't mean that you have to be best friends with every person, but be willing to know them well enough to see what motivates them.

When you understand the fears of those around you, it will give you an insight into your own fears and how they influence the way you work and relate to others at work.

If fear motivates you to earn money for its own sake, then you create more fear. Many people crave financial security and status, believing that with these things they will be happy. But the fear that motivates such cravings – fear of poverty, fear of being without status – actually creates obstacles to achieving serenity.

To find serenity in your workplace, and contentment with your role, begin to regard your work as a pathway to self-knowledge. Work is a spiritual experience, whether it is pleasant or unpleasant, satisfying or dull, degrading or enriching. If you approach your work with a desire for self-knowledge, you will soon discover whether your current work situation is an expression of fear or a confirmation of your inner wellbeing. And at the same time the way other people behave at work expresses their inner state.

It is important to know that, even if it appears otherwise, you have choices about the work you do and the way you do it. If you feel trapped, you can free yourself. If you feel fearful for any reason in the workplace, you need to isolate the origin of this fear. Whether it stems from a situation, a person or an atmosphere, you must find the power of the fear and turn it into a positive force. You can do this using the following exercise:

In your mind's eye, see a great roaring fire. Take the fear and cast it in, giving it all up to the fire. Let the fire consume it and reduce it to essence. As this happens, the fear is transforming, showing you where it comes from and why. Allow the answer to flow into your heart, then let this feeling take the form of a solution and a course of action. Do this for ten days consecutively and you will heal this fear.

To begin to awaken the serenity within you and within your workplace is very simple. Start by giving thanks, regularly each day, for all that you have within the workplace, for what you earn and for all that you do, regardless of what it is. Serenity is not concerned with status, importance or workload. By doing this, you will begin to awaken the energy of serenity that exists in you, in your colleagues and within the workplace itself. You will soon notice the atmosphere change as calm, happiness and natural vitality blossom.

2. LOVE, MERCY AND GRACE

As love is the fuel of the human soul, so mercy is the energy that gives us the chance to forgive and move into a state of grace, the natural spiritual state that occurs within us when we are aligned with inner love. Grace is the energy that expresses mercy in all our interactions with people. And at the heart of grace is serenity.

Love exists in all of us and is our most powerful connection to other people, but love is surrounded by fear in many guises. We fear loving and being loved; we fear rejection, abandonment and betrayal; we fear trusting and becoming close. Sometimes fear even drives us to pretend to love another person. But while there are fears surrounding love, in love itself there is no fear, nor is there any pretence, for love is not ours to direct, and when we do truly love, it leads us to serenity.

Love lasts for ever. It changes direction and, from time to time, form. It grows and moves on, but once you have really loved someone, that love will always be there. Each one of us must find the courage to accept love when it comes to us, and love always comes; it does not abandon anyone. The greatest thing that can happen to any of us in the everyday world is to love and be loved in return. The path to love begins by allowing kindness into your life and sharing kindness with other people. Love seeks to be given freely and every one of us can be loved and loving.

Love can appear in many different kinds of relationship with other people, including the love a marriage partner has for another, the love between parent and child, the love between friends and spiritual love. It is by loving that we make the world and find out what we are really made of.

The fears surrounding love appear because love makes us feel vulnerable, and for many people to feel vulnerable is fearful. Yet to fear love is to fear life, and to fear life is to fear the gift of serenity and to turn away from life. Yet when we accept love, we move into the greater knowing; we understand that we are connected to all life and that in this lies the essence of serenity.

3. ANGER AND ANXIETY

Every one of us feels anger at times, but it is an emotion to be wary of. Anger shrinks us and contaminates us, keeping us poor and fearful. It kills love and keeps us distant from other people.

Anger is a signal we must listen to. When you are angry, it is a sign that something needs to change. Listen to it and make the change, but do not simply stay angry. Those who are angry for much of the time are blocking their own paths to spiritual development. You cannot transform fear into serenity while you are angry. So when anger rises in you, do nothing to feed it. Choose instead to dissolve it with loving kindness.

If you are around another person who is constantly angry, then protect yourself by moving away from them, at the same time sending them the energy of love and forgiveness.

You cannot fight anger with force. Loving patience is far more effective. Impatience, which leads to anger, breeds anxiety, fear, discouragement and failure. Patience creates confidence, decisiveness and a generous attitude, which leads to success.

4. ILLNESS

Are you afraid of other people's illness? Stop and think about this and consider why. Does their suffering scare you? Are you afraid that you will get sick? If they are in pain, will you feel it? Do you want to avoid pain at any cost? That is natural. However, all of this is fear, fear of understanding yourself in contact with your fellow human being. When we are afraid of the illness of others, we are afraid of becoming ill and dying ourselves. Fear seeks to create separation and prejudice. We should learn from all forms of illness and understand it as a pathway to self-knowledge and the transformation of fear. If we are not afraid in this way, it means we are at peace with the cycles of material suffering and understand our own fears well enough to move beyond them.

5. FAMILY

Our family is a group of people to whom we are deeply connected. But this connection is not solely created by blood ties; it is created by loving and caring. So our true family is made up of those people we care most deeply about. If these are also blood relatives, then we are doubly blessed because we have a special connection with those to whom we are physically related, since it is through them that we seek to know who we are. We don't always get on with our birth families. Many families squabble and fall out, but family fights and feuds are simply unskilful expressions of the desire to know who we are. Sometimes we have a fear of being part of a family and we reject or move away from our birth families. The fear of being part of a family is the fear of not belonging, of being cast aside from love, and it can also be a spur that prompts us to find the family that we truly belong to. In time, as we gather a family of our choice, we are able to look back and begin to appreciate and understand our birth families far more. When we do this, we start to connect with the wider human family, and as we do, the fear of feeling part of a family dissolves. The family we choose is the family in which our soul can learn its life's lessons best, while our birth family shows us the lessons we have learnt and the lessons and behaviour we need to unlearn.

6. FRIENDSHIP

Friendship is a powerful blessing that brings both love and respect into our lives. And the joy of friendship is that it is straightforward and relatively simple to achieve; to have a friend, you must be one. Offer friendship to others and they will be instantly drawn to you. Never wait for friendship to come to you; you can make more friends in a week by becoming interested in other people than you can in a year by trying to get other people to be interested in you.

Friendship is also a clue to the character of others. When the character of a person is not clear to you, look at this person's friends. If a person is honest and open, they will have good friends who respect and trust them.

Spending time with friends is both enriching and enlightening. There are few things better in life than spending a few hours in conversation with people you respect and love. And in making time to talk, as long as you are genuine in what you say, you will discover more about how your heart is working, what matters to you and the path you wish to take.

When someone allows you to bear their burdens, you have found deep friendship and such a friendship will not be affected by the ups and downs of life, events and emotions. The friendship that can instantly cease has never been real.

There is a skill in choosing friends who are trustworthy and constant. We need to cultivate in ourselves the qualities we wish for in friends, and to give ourselves time to recognise who is worthy of trust. Sometimes, when we are let down or betrayed by a friend, we feel we have made a mistake or exercised poor judgement. When this happens, understand that this person has come into your life to bring you a valuable lesson. Rather than condemning yourself for your choice, or them for what they have done to you, look for the lesson in the experience.

7. SELF-ESTEEM

People think that self-esteem is confidence or positive thinking or the ability to get on with life when things are tough. But these are only part of the story. True self-esteem knows how to be in the right place at the right time. This is not based on ego or seizing the moment for selfish ends but rather on a connection with love that moves in harmony with the natural cycles of life. This wise form of self-esteem is free from fear and enables you to be responsible for your thoughts, deeds and actions. It is not projection of the ego but the opposite – the acknowledgement of the soul and its effect upon the world as a real force. Such self-esteem is the sacredness of life, applied to the everyday events that we experience. Each of us has this self-esteem. It connects us all, brings us friends, gives us lovers, husbands, wives and children. You can feel it in others when you allow your heart to be open to other people.

8. INTEGRITY

Our lives improve only when we take chances – and the truest and most difficult risk we can take is to be honest with ourselves. When we are we create integrity, which is the direct action of the soul upon the world. Integrity is the energy behind change and the energy of change itself.

Change has a huge emotional impact on the human consciousness. To the fearful, it is threatening because it means that things may get worse. To the hopeful, it is encouraging because things may get better. To the confident, it is inspiring because the challenge exists to make things better. Integrity is the honourable and elegant use of change. By staying true to yourself as everything around you changes, you come through change without diminishing your inner knowledge of what is true, moral and natural.

When we have a lack of integrity, we lose our natural connection to others and become isolated, and the more we stay this way, the more we look outside of ourselves.

9. FORGIVENESS

Each time we truly forgive, a little more goodness comes into the world. Forgiveness takes courage, self-knowledge, self-love and serenity. The ability to forgive is the attribute of the truly strong. It is easy to say that you are a forgiving person until you are faced with having to forgive a deep hurt or wound inflicted by another person. Life is an adventure in forgiveness.

Forgiveness is the healing of wounds, however they may be caused. It does not always lead to healed relationships, but it does lead to healed lives. When you choose to let go of a past wrong and of blame and hatred, you choose to invite love and peace into your life.

It really does not matter whether the person who hurt you deserves to be forgiven. Forgiveness is a gift you give yourself because when you forgive, you release yourself from a burden of pain and bitterness. When you forgive, you heal your fear, from that comes serenity, and in that lives contentment. Contentment has no fear and is an expression of serenity that most people can sense and relate to. Contentment is mature happiness. It seeks nothing and cannot be reduced by circumstance.

If your life is affected by someone who refuses to forgive, or is not capable of forgiveness, wish them well and then let them go from your life, along with your anger.

10. SPIRITUAL DEVELOPMENT

Spiritual development is a wondrous thing, yet many still find it hard to develop the spiritual aspect of their lives. There are many paths that can be taken to do this, but here is a simple way to develop your own spirituality:

1. Cultivate simplicity.
2. Understand the nature of faith in your life.
3. Develop and understand freedom and self-reliance.

Spend time on these three steps and all forms of spiritual potential will bring themselves to you in peace, direct experience and balance. So often, through fear and misunderstanding, people divorce their spiritual development from their daily lives. Do not be afraid to live the life you want, to develop spirituality and to follow your dreams. The first step, to cultivate simplicity, will begin to invite your dreams into your life. As you simplify your life, the laws of the universe and the cycles of your own life will be more easily understood. Simplicity is the height of civilisation and the way to create it is to let go of the excess baggage in your life and concentrate on what is truly important. The world is full of treasures and of good people. Concentrate on these and on the beauty in life and let go of that which causes you stress and unhappiness.

Some think that having faith means being convinced that what they believe in, whatever that may be, exists in the same way a table exists. Those who cannot be completely convinced of the existence of a spiritual truth think faith is impossible for them. If this is you, then be assured that you can have doubts and have faith at the same time. In fact, people who doubt can have great faith because faith is not something you think, not a set of logical conclusions, but something that you are, that you live and breathe. The greater your doubts, the more serene your faith will become when you allow it into your life. And this in turn will bring you the gift of freedom.

The most precious gift of all – freedom – is one we hold in our hearts. We have within us the freedom to express our souls, our love and the truth that we know and have daily experience of the divine. This gives us the freedom to be who we want to be. We are already free but we easily forget that we are. Do not give that freedom away and no one will be able to take it from you. In order to make sure your experience of freedom can survive the rigours of daily life, you have to develop inner and outer self-reliance. Self-reliance is the first step to lasting freedom, and this teaches you that being one's own person is its ultimate reward.

11. DAILY LIVING

For many people, the biggest challenge that they face is the day in front of them when they wake. To live consciously and in harmony with the day and all that it may bring you is a major emotional and spiritual achievement. Yet for many, this seems an impossibility. Their days are clouded with confusion, annoyance, exhaustion and upsets, which make harmony seem out of reach. Each one of us needs to look at how we live each day and why we live the way we do. If your day is a mystery, if you wonder where it all went at the end of the day, take time to find out. Try to examine how your day starts, what happens in the middle of the day and how it ends before you sleep. Examine what thoughts you have, attitudes and habits. When you do, you will realise how much your daily life is affected by the actions of other people. There are countless cycles and events, seen and unseen, in our daily lives that are run or affected by other people that we do not know. For instance, the power in our homes, the food that we buy and eat, the websites we use on the internet and the traffic jam we get into on the way home all involve other people. In our modern society it is, paradoxically, easy to forget that we are more dependent now on other people than we were in the past, even though our personal connections with other people are often less satisfactory.

The challenge of daily life is not to just overcome issues, problems and obstacles but to transform them into blessings. Blessings take care of themselves, while problems beg for attention. If your day is filled with problems, begin to make changes by looking at your own reactions to events. Are you problem-spotting instead of noticing the blessings that come your way? Do you take for granted all the things that happen easily and run smoothly and the little acts of kindness that you receive from others? They will be there if you are willing to spot them. And the more good things you notice, the less space in your day there will be for problems and difficulties. Choose to make the way you live your daily life an act of harmony and bring daily blessings into your life.

I sat there on the hill, gazing into space.

'What do I do about other people and all their problems, Ürgyen? How do I make sense of it all?'

My teacher sat looking thoughtfully down into the valley.

'There are no other people,' he said. 'It is the separation within our own lives and from ourselves that creates the idea of other people being different. People are the same, and their cycles of experience are also the same. We must trust this. By becoming whole within ourselves, we claim back the differences and we claim back our lives. Then there are no others. We become real individuals who are a willing part of other people's shared experiences. We become connected through love and wisdom. All the fear goes and we are content with what we have. Our foundation is serenity. We are part of each other. We are responsible each to the other, and in that for ourselves.'

GUIDANCE IN KNOWING OTHERS

What follows are twelve simple sets of guidelines that will help you to observe and understand other people. Apply them to your daily life and use them to know yourself and others. Each set of guidelines is divided into three. The number three affects mind, body and intellect, bringing clarity of mind and peacefulness.

1. THE THREE EXPRESSIONS OF INTELLIGENCE

In your daily relationships with people always remember that there are three basic expressions of intelligence that we all have within us:

The first works things out for itself.
The second recognises the value of what others can understand.
The third cannot grasp anything for itself or by the example of others.

The first expression is admirable, the second is of high calibre, and the third can be wasteful. By observing and knowing the cycles of these three within yourself, you will begin to see them clearly in other people. This will be of value in all your dealings in the world and will help you to show love and direction and to encourage others to do their best. Other people want to tell you a story, the story of what they are worth, and their hopes and fears are often expressed through these three aspects of intelligence.

2. THE THREE CLASSES OF HUMANITY

All humanity divides itself into these three classes:

Those people who are fixed in their ways and behaviour. They take charge of life. They wish to achieve.
Those who are changeable, moment to moment, reflecting life back at others. They wish to be part of life's cycles.

Those who are not either of the first two but feel that life is a battle. They feel overwhelmed by life, and fear affects them more than the first two.

3. THE THREE FACETS OF A PRECIOUS LIFE

In your daily life cultivate the three facets that you need to create a precious life for yourself and for others:

Firstly, be open to learning and always encourage others to do the same.
Secondly, be open to earning your way in the world and help others to do the same.
Thirdly, do not be shy of yearning for the beautiful and true in your life and help others to see beauty within themselves.

4. THE THREE EXCELLENT ATTITUDES

Throughout your life do your best to keep to these three excellent attitudes:

Think good thoughts.
Speak good words.
Make every action and deed a good one.

5. THE THREE STATES

Beliefs that we hold dear are often tested to the limit by the attitudes of others. Many will go through one or more of the following states. Remember that this is a good thing as it will only help you to clarify your beliefs.

Firstly, other people will say it conflicts with their sensitivities, beliefs or religion.

Secondly, other people will say it has been discovered before. Thirdly, other people will say they have always believed it.

Remember, other people will always want to believe what you believe just so they can own something, to have some sense of control and belonging. Always allow your beliefs to be adaptable, but your experience and understanding to be solid.

6. THE THREE PRIME WAYS

In gaining knowledge of yourself, the world and other people, there are three prime ways:

The first is the observation of people, yourself and nature.
The second is reflection on what you have observed.
The third is taking your observations and applying them to the world at large.

Observation assembles verification of what you have observed, reflection merges them, and application reveals whether the first two are useful. In establishing these prime ways, you will gain insight into the behaviour and habits of other people.

7. THE THREE QUESTIONS

From the three prime ways you can move on to asking three questions, which we have, in the very process of living, no choice but to answer:

What is right or wrong in my life?
What is true or false in my life?
What in my life is inspired, and what is painful?

Look at your own life to answer these questions. Your answers will give you information about what changes you might wish to make in your life. In applying the questions as you observe others, you will come to understand better what is happening in their lives.

8. THE THREE KINDS OF PEOPLE

In life people place themselves into three groups. Each of these three groups is driven by the desire to feel alive, to be safe, secure and whole.

The small number of people who make things happen.
The much larger number who expect those things that happen.
The vast majority who have no idea whether anything happened.

Which group are you in, and which would you like to be in? Look at the people around you – which group is each of them in? By observing each of these groups of people, you will discover how their fear controls them, directs them and creates the life they have and the society that they live in.

9. THE THREE THINGS WE SHOULD TRY TO DO EVERY DAY

Laugh – at ourselves and then with others, but never at others.
Reflect – on inspiring ideas, be still and meditate on serenity.
Empathise – with your fellow human beings. Allow your emotions to enriched with all the experiences of others around you, allow yourself to be moved to tears, to feel companionship and to extend compassion and warmth.

In the course of a day if you can laugh, reflect and

empathise, then you have had a perfect day and your own lesson in the miraculous.

10. THE THREE QUALITIES TO POSSESS

When you stop to look at yourself and wonder how others see you, be sure that they will see in you the following qualities:

Generosity in all your thoughts and actions.
Humanity in your dealing with other people.
Self-control in the expression of your own success.

11. THE THREE IMPULSES OF THE SOUL

There are three impulses of the soul that need to be fulfilled:

The first is that of the affluent person who wants something extra.
The second is that of the sick person who wants anything different to what they are experiencing.
The third is that of the visitor who exclaims, often silently, that they would rather be somewhere other than where they are.

These three come from each person's deep understanding that everything is fleeting. We all have these impulses. We need to learn how they are of value to us so that we may recognise them in ourselves or in others, and thereby be thankful for the life we have and not become caught up solely in the 'bubble' of our own lives.

12. THE THREE PASSIONS

There are three passions, simple but overwhelmingly strong,

that can make sense of this fleeting life. They have guided my life, and I believe you may find them helpful.

The first is the hopefulness of love in all its forms. Love presents itself in many faces, and if we are brave we can see it in all its forms and welcome it into our beings.

The second is the courage to accept all forms of wisdom, wherever it may come from, and not to think that wisdom comes from one source only.

The third is of your own free will to enter into the suffering of humankind and help to ease it, enabling others to raise their heads to know they too are worthy of humanity. How do you enter into the suffering of humankind? The most direct and simple way is to understand that other people's suffering is in fact your own. We are all part of the cycle of suffering and freedom from the suffering made by fear, for it is fear that makes suffering possible.

All of these principles enable us to understand other people and thereby understand ourselves, heal fear, be courageous and become full of humanity and kindness. They are stepping stones that each of us can use to become those people who walk lightly through dark and difficult times. They are aids to navigate life's difficulties and to make our life's journey with ease and skill.

4
INNER POWER

This chapter is about power and control, both in the world around us and, most importantly, internally, over your varying states of mind.

When you have command over your state of mind, you have great power. You are able to choose how to approach any situation in your life, for with inner power comes outer power – power over your behaviour and actions and thus influence over others.

Through gentle reflection and absorption of the information that follows, you will come to understand how you can be in command of your inner and outer states. Serenity is at the heart of this process, and by following the steps in this chapter, you will come to know how to have direct experience of serenity in every aspect of your daily life.

The result will be that when the issues of power and control present themselves in your life, even in those fragile times when you are powerless and have no control, you will look into the face of your own inner power and not be afraid.

THE SIXTEEN MEDITATIONS ON POWER

To begin the process of discovering your inner power, I would like you to look at the following sixteen meditations, which take the form of affirmations and questions. Speak each of them aloud slowly, for by doing this, you will invoke their potential in you and awaken your inner power. Think about them deeply and reflect upon them, absorbing their message.

The number sixteen has a special significance within Bön in that it is believed that if you study a subject in sixteen different ways, you will understand it better.

1. If it were true that absolute power corrupts absolutely, would absolute powerlessness make you pure? Are you brave enough to be powerless?

2. One of the great secrets of power is never to misuse the impulse behind your power when trying to make something happen. It is best to do no more than you can. Know what is appropriate.

3. Be ready for more than the life you are now living.

4. Tell all the people that you know that you have more power than you are at this moment drawing on. Study their reactions. Be sure to do this in a kind way and do not be boastful with it. Everyone has more power than they ever use or understand.

5. If you do not fill up and spill over the place in your life that you currently occupy, you are living small and hiding. The inner power that is you and that fuels your life will always give you more. The skill is to use the extra wisely.

6. The first stride in reaching for the things you want out of life is this: decide what it is that you truly want, then throw out all that is unnecessary.

7. Not a shred of evidence exists in support of the idea that life is serious. Life is too important to take seriously. People confuse seriousness with the coldness and unskilful control of power based on fear. True seriousness is happiness immersed in serenity.

8. Do you consider life to be a foreign language that everyone mispronounces, saying it is impossible to learn? Stop this, surrender and let life speak through you.

9. Life celebrates itself by its own actions in which people play an unimportant part.

10. People have too many grand-sounding words and too few actions that correspond with them.

11. We arrive, at some point in our lives, at an outermost edge caused by our own actions. When we are there we may find it fearful because our everyday mind does not know what to do. When this happens, we must stop doing what we have been doing and accept that our fears are the product of the everyday world and only the serene within us will suffice.

12. All human actions in the everyday world have one or more of these seven causes: chance, nature, compulsion, habit, reason, passion and desire. Yet it is only love that makes sense of them all, releasing their power and giving you self-control.

13. People absorb particular qualities by constantly acting a specific way, so if you have the mental intent, you can

become just by carrying out just actions: gentle by expressing gentleness, courageous by showing courage.

14. Do not be too timid and squeamish about your actions.

15. All life is research. The more research you do, the better.

16. Strong reasons create strong actions.

Now, in the light of these meditations, take some time to reflect on your personal history to extract the value of the lessons of the past. Look at moments in your life when you did not use the power you had, when you perhaps held back for the good of others. Did you gain a sense of wellbeing or completion within yourself? Were there other times when you had power over others and used it unfairly, or in a thought-less way? If you gain the skill of knowing when not to use all your power, you will lead and inspire others far more creatively, effectively and fairly. Nearly all people can deal with misfortune, but if you want to test a person's character, give them power. It does not matter what the power or what the situation, you will gain great insight from observing the way the person uses their power. Are they compassionate, fair and generous? Or are they heavy-handed, over-zealous and uncaring? Do they relish power arrogantly, enjoy it wisely, or fear having it and hold back from using it at all?

Power is holding another's fear in your hand and showing it to them. The only reason to have power and the only benefit of it is the ability to do good, and this takes courage. To understand the pains of power, you must go to those who have it; to know its pleasures, we must go to those who are seeking it.

People say that power corrupts, but it would be more true to say that power attracts the easily led and those who are already corrupted with false values and selfish goals. Wise and balanced people, those who know the truth of life, are usually concerned with things other than power. They know and understand that the only power worth having is the power that lies within each one of us, waiting to be awakened.

THE SIXTEEN MEDITATIONS ON BALANCED INNER POWER

Do you want to discover your inner power? Below are listed the sixteen different aspects of balanced inner power. As you have meditated on the sixteen points on pages 77–79, please contemplate each of the sixteen below and allow them to enter your heart and awaken your inner power.

1. CONFIDENCE

Every human being has the potential for great inner power, and awakening this potential begins with building confidence. Each one of us can do extraordinary things if we have inner confidence. Yet most people lead cautious, fearful lives, more willing to sit back and watch others' achievements on television than to attempt to achieve in their own lives.

To begin to awaken the confidence within you, repeat over and over to yourself: *It all depends on me.* Then, having decided to achieve a particular task, push yourself to achieve it, even if doing so is tedious, distasteful, difficult or discouraging. Accomplishing a task, particularly when it is tiresome or challenging, brings with it the gift of greater self-confidence. You know, from then on, that you have the resilience and determination in you to achieve what you set your mind to.

Attempt easy tasks as if they were difficult and difficult as if they were easy; in the one case that confidence may not fall asleep, in the other that it may not be dismayed. The person who has confidence in themself gains the confidence of others. So believe in yourself and have faith in your abilities. Without a humble but reasonable confidence in your own powers, you cannot be successful or happy.

Every time you do not follow your inner guidance, you lose energy, and every time you do not listen to yourself, you give away your power to others, often those who do not deserve it and will misuse it. It is only good to give power away if there is a benefit in such an action and this is rarely true.

When you have confidence, you have drive and determination, and these will take you further in life than talent or ability.

2. SUCCESS

On the path to success your decision to succeed is more important than anything else. But before you decide to chase success, be sure you understand what it is and why you want it. Success for its own sake is meaningless. It is far better to aim to become a person of honesty, spiritual awareness and humanity, for these are the ingredients of true success. It is possible to fail in many ways, while there is only one way to truly succeed – an unconditional acceptance of life and what it brings. When you achieve this, every experience you have is successful.

The sure way to be unsuccessful is to try to please everybody. Avoid this and keep your focus on yourself and the purpose and meaning behind your actions. Know that you are a success if you can get up in the morning and go to bed at night having in between done what you wanted to do while bringing goodness to others.

Material success in life is not wrong or distasteful if you approach it and manage it with the right attitude. But be sure that you aren't overwhelmed and taken in by it. If your success is not on your own terms, if it appears to the world attractive and glamorous but you do not trust it in your heart, it is not success at all. Success comes from self-knowledge, and the man or woman who makes a success of living is the one who perceives the ambition as having already taken place then steadily aims for it, gathering it in, as if it were a net.

In the world of work real success is discovering a job that has meaning for you and doing it with loving energy. This energy then goes back into your work and so enriches the world. And in life you have achieved success when you know in your soul that you have lived as well as you could, based on what you knew of yourself at the time, laughed often, showed kindness to all and loved much.

3. FAILURE

Good people are good because they have achieved wisdom through failure. They have learnt to accept that failure is an unavoidable part of life and need carry no sense of shame or loss, for to fail you must have tried.

Failure is what happens when we need to learn faith in the world and ourselves. If we learn nothing from failure, then we continue to fail – and to chase perfection, believing that 'next time' we will achieve it. But try as hard as we might to achieve perfection, the result of our labours is always an amazing variety of imperfections. We may see these imperfections as failures, but each of them holds divine lessons and brings us beauty, and if we are able to discover this, we grow in self-knowledge and move closer to the true success that is acceptance.

People who consider themselves, or are considered by others, to be failures in life are simply those who did not become conscious of just how close they were to success when they gave up. Be brave in picking yourself up and carrying on after a failure, knowing that if you accept that failure as an unavoidable and valuable part of life, then you are a step closer to success.

4. WORRY

If you adopt the habit of worrying every day about things you cannot change or which might never happen, all you will achieve is ill health, tension and unhappiness. Regularly thinking about what worries you for a single instant too long is the most effective way of hurting yourself emotionally.

Under the influence of fear, which has become part of our culture, we have come to believe that it is realistic to be negative and unrealistic to approach life's concerns with positive energy and love. We have taught ourselves to expect the worst. How often do people say, as they list all kinds of negative possibilities, 'I'm only trying to be realistic'? Yet there is just as much possibility that things will turn out well. The universe has an abundance of positive energy, if we are willing to tap into it by believing that all will be well.

To transform worry into contentment, activate the light of your inner power and fill your heart with love. Sit quietly and focus on love filling your body, your heart and your mind. If you allow love to be in your consciousness, your worries will not harm you, and you will begin to dissolve them. Love will show you how to solve your worries and will remind you of the joy of contentment and peace.

In order to release yourself from worry on a daily basis, end each day in thanks and stillness and then release it, along with any worries it brought, knowing that during the day you have done your best. Some errors and absurdity no doubt presented themselves; learn from them and disregard them as soon as you can. Tomorrow will be a brand-new experience. Begin it well, serene and with your spirit full of energy, hope and courage, ready to do your best once more.

When we lose confidence in life, in ourselves and in other people, when we feel hopeless, depressed, defeated and overwhelmed by worry and doubt, then we are going in a direction that is counter to the universe. This means that we make life far harder for ourselves. It's as if we are wading through thick mud, instead of skipping along – in other words, a perpetually negative state of mind will in the end create a hard and disappointing life.

To change this, start by insisting, kindly and firmly, to yourself and others, on being yourself. Under no circumstances try to be like anyone else. You are irreplaceable, rare and incomparable. You need not try to safeguard your integrity and dignity, for if your heart is strong, they will be safe and will protect you. By being yourself, you will access your inner power and develop self-respect and self-love, both vital aspects of real confidence.

5. THOUGHT

The thoughts that we have are very powerful, whether we know it or not. So when we learn to control our thoughts, we have achieved great inner power.

Each person's thoughts connect them with all other people,

and so the energy of thought is enormous. A thought is not just a small, private awareness that disappears, but a unit of energy, which remains present in the world and has an effect on everything around us. Therefore it is vital to choose your thoughts with care. Thoughts not only carry themselves to others, but they lead us to our behaviour and actions. So choose to let negative, unkind or self-defeating thoughts go. Concentrate on thoughts that support yourself and others in leading good lives and achieving peace and contentment.

Nothing in the world is as sacred as the integrity of your own mind. When you truly experience this for yourself, you have achieved inner power.

When we take time to see the influence of our thoughts, and subsequent actions, upon our loved ones, friends, family and even enemies, we understand that what has passed behind us and what may be before us are insignificant compared to what lies within us.

Use the power of your thoughts wisely, use it to connect yourself to others, to achieve your dreams and to believe in yourself.

6. POSITIVE ATTITUDE

It takes determination to maintain a positive frame of mind and attitude in the face of what appears to be defeat, loss or hurt. Yet to cultivate inner power, it is important to remain positive, whatever your situation. If you can be cheerful and optimistic in the direst of circumstances, then you have indeed achieved inner power and you have understood that the greater part of your happiness or misery depends upon your temperament, not upon your circumstances. And temperament is not, as some people think, a given, like hair colour, but is something we have a choice in determining and can influence through our behaviour and attitudes.

A strong positive mental attitude can bring about miracles, leading to both inner and outer healing for ourselves and for others around us. The great spiritual leaders of the past and present, in all religions and spiritual disciplines, have all had in common an attitude positive enough to find blessings in suffering and to maintain their beliefs and integrity in the face of doubt and dissent.

By altering your mental attitude, you can change your life. In fact, when you wish to make changes, mental attitude is everything. If you plan to run a marathon, learn new skills, lose weight or meet the partner of your dreams, what will count most in achieving success is your mental attitude. If you believe you can do it, no matter what setbacks you meet, then you will do it. To transform your life, first transform your attitude and then watch out for miracles!

7. HABITS

In order to support the release of your inner power and serenity, you need to change any habits that are holding you back or affecting you adversely. We all have habits: human beings are habit-forming creatures and find comfort and stability in repetitive behaviour. Many of our habits are useful, constructive and necessary, but never take any habit for granted – always be willing to examine habits and decide whether they are useful or valuable to you or not. That way, you control your habits, they don't control you.

Bad habits have a destructive effect on your life, on your confidence and on your energy. If you habitually smoke, drink to excess, take drugs, overspend or treat yourself or others cruelly, then you need to stop. Good habits result from resisting temptation.

Releasing a bad habit is not simply a question of deciding to stop. Habits become very deeply ingrained and often have a physical effect on the body. So coax your habit out of your life a step at a time, supported by the one thing that is stronger than habit – the power of kindness to the self. Once you have made the decision to be kind to yourself, your unskilful habits will gladly change.

8. INTELLIGENCE

True intelligence is revolutionary and wondrous. It is not the mindless regurgitation of others' ideas, which often passes for education. It is not slyness, quickness or approval-seeking. Nor is it to be found in an over-active mind, which is simply a reactive mind, affected by all that comes to it, to the point that it becomes no mind at all but simply a mindless habit.

Real intelligence is the capacity to fearlessly focus awareness on what is genuinely important. It is based on inner power, that is the ability to trust your own knowledge, beliefs and observations, and it is compassionate, unifying, decisive and relentless.

Real intelligence is uncompromising in its challenge to the status quo. It questions everything and gazes into all the dimensions of Hell and Heaven without fear.

Such intelligence is immeasurable and illuminates the world by its radiance. According to the Tibetan Bön tradition, it is the brilliant light of intelligence that generates our central nervous system and our brain waves. This intelligence moves not just in our brains but also beyond the confines of our bodies, affecting other people and our environment directly.

Cultivate your own intelligence, and the inner power that supports it, by refusing to accept mindless reactivity. Ask questions, draw your own conclusions, know what you think and be brave in stating it.

9. OPPORTUNITIES

Life is full of opportunities, and opportunities are windows of hope, possibility and joy. For an opportunity to blossom into a successful outcome requires the right place, the right time and the right frame of mind.

There are two kinds of opportunity – those we see and take advantage of and those we generate ourselves. Be aware of both and enjoy them. Allow your inner power to guide you towards the right opportunities in your life, as well as help you create them.

Remember that the obstacles in your life are often only opportunities in a different guise. When we pause to doubt our inner power, we habitually miss opportunities. Use inner power in every activity in your daily life, taking part in that activity with conscious intent and a positive attitude, and you will attract increased good fortune and opportunities. And next time there is a crisis in your life, try to identify the opportunity that it offers, even if at first it is very hard to recognise.

Do not be afraid, at certain times of your life, to walk alone. If you blindly follow the crowd, you will get no further than the crowd. When you trust your inner direction, you will find yourself discovering new places, your inner power will be awakened and your heart will be alive to new life.

As you create and take the opportunities that come to you, do not be afraid to make mistakes. Each time we refuse to admit to an error, we erode a little of our individuality and our inner power. Be brave, also, about making decisions. To move forward with the opportunities in our lives, we must make decisions. The more clear and courageous you are about this, the more it will strengthen your inner power. Being indecisive erodes energy and simply returns you to the starting point – having to make the decision.

To create opportunities, you need to have dreams. A dream is different from a desire. Desire is the impulse, but the dream happens when you build your desire into an emotional and energetic structure. (At the end of the chapter you will learn a powerful method for doing this.)

When you allow yourself to dream, you begin to create great ideas. Never worry about people stealing them, for no one can steal the energy of the ideas and therefore stolen ideas lose most of their potency. To immerse yourself in your inner power, chase each one of your dreams. Look forward to everything, expect nothing, live from your heart and the world will give you what you want.

10. OPTIMISM

Consistent optimism expands and amplifies your thoughts and willpower, increases your inner power and teaches the benefits of self-control, for to be consistently optimistic requires conscious choice and effort.

Optimism, like the season of spring, is about rebirth, regeneration and renewal, and if you are an optimist, then it makes all your dealings with people and events much easier. Optimism is infectious; it rubs off on others who respond warmly and find their own outlook becoming more optimistic.

Optimism is not about ignorance or blind faith but more about believing in the best possible outcome for any situation or course of action. Cultivate your own optimism as the most valuable approach to take in life and the surest way of developing inner power.

11. TAKING RISKS

Read the meditation below and reflect upon it for a time. Breathe in, be the flower, be its perfume.

A MEDITATION ON RISK

The little flower was afraid. The day came when the risk of remaining closed away from the world, as a bud, was more agonising than the risk of blossoming. The flower bloomed. It gasped and then gave out such perfume that it filled the air with its happiness. Suddenly, all the other flowers bloomed as well, inspired by the little flower. What had been a rocky, soulless place became for a short time a garden of wonder and wisdom.

Life should not be measured in the number of years you have lived but rather in the quality of the life you have led. Happiness does not come from leading a long life but from facing challenges and taking risks.

It is through taking risks that we learn how truly powerful we are, as we learn to control and direct the events and energy that have been released by the risks we have taken.

I don't mean that you should take reckless or rash risks for their own sake. I am referring to the calculated risks that are part of living life to the full. These include the risk of loving and being loved, the risk of committing to another, the risk of taking on a challenge that excites you, the risk of exploring the world and discovering its beauty and the risk of standing up for what you believe in.

When a risk you have taken goes wrong, bless the situation and move on. Don't let it put you off further risks. For instance, if a relationship has failed, don't hide away licking your wounds and refusing ever to risk another relationship. Caution will close you down. In your desire for safety you will lose the vitality that creates life's wonders and that blesses the opportunity to take a chance. You will become an observer of life and not a participant, and to do this is to submit to fear.

It is through taking risks that your inner power is awakened. When you do this, you will understand that real safety comes from the forging of power and control deep within the fires of your inner self.

Do not be put off by the opinions of others when they say, 'That's impossible.' Do the most difficult thing on earth for you. Sometimes we have to jump off our own personal cliffs in order to test ourselves to the limit and strengthen our inner power.

The universe will reward you for taking risks, for risks taken in this way help to aid the emotional and spiritual evolution of every human being. Taking a risk is being willing to make a change, and it is the forces of change that fill the world with meaning.

12. IMAGINATION

Imagination is more essential than knowledge, for it is the operating energy of your inner world. And whereas knowledge is, by its nature, never complete, imagination is perfect, whole and complete in each one of us.

Imagination is the tool we can use to bring joy and peace to the world. Filled with never-ending energy, imagination establishes the desire for friendship and connection. With our imagination we can make the leap from being separate to being part of a whole; we can connect with every other living being on the planet and know that the difference between past, present and future is merely a false impression. Imagination is vibrant, loving and is born of inner power. With imagination we can help the world to become a better place, in which people work together for freedom and a spirit of tolerance and love.

Feed your imagination by strengthening your inner power. Heal your fear and allow imagination to stretch the bounds of knowledge and encourage freedom of expression for you and for all peoples.

13. KINDNESS, BEAUTY AND TRUTH

As you travel through life, take with you these three ideals – kindness, beauty and truth. Allow them to light your way and to give you fresh courage to face life when obstacles and difficulties litter your path. As we develop our inner power, we come to understand the importance of these three ideals far more. We recognise that when you are kind to another, you spread kindness in the world, when you recognise beauty, you add to the beauty in the world, and when you seek and speak the truth, you add to the truthfulness in the world. Powerful in its simplicity, this recognition is a beacon to live by.

Allow the kindness, beauty and truth in you to surface and to show you the way forward when times are difficult. Live your life for yourself but live it for others too. This will bring a new sense of value to your life and will bring you balance, serenity and peace.

14. CURIOSITY

One cannot help but be filled with awe and curiosity when one contemplates the mysteries of eternity, of life and of the marvellous structure of reality. Curiosity, the instinctive desire to know and understand more of life's mysteries, is part of what makes us human.

Never lose your holy curiosity. It is your ability to pause in wonder or stand rapt in awe, and without it we are mere automatons. The most beautiful thing we can experience is the mysterious. Life is richer if we try to comprehend a little of its mystery every day.

Curiosity is also the source of all true art and science. It is a vital element of the most important human endeavour of all, the striving for morality in our actions. Our inner balance and even our very existence depend on it, for only morality in our actions can give beauty and dignity to life.

15. INTUITION

The most valuable asset we have in our daily life is intuition. Yet in today's world intuition is often considered far less valuable than thought. We live in an age in which the logic of thinking is prized far more highly than the feeling of intuition. Despite this, we all have in us a powerful sense of intuition, which we can nurture and grow, for intuition is made and renewed by the experience of truth and beauty in your daily life.

Intuition lies behind personal creativity and ability and gives us information that defies logic. Trust your intuition when it tells you something that you feel certain is right or true. All too often we are encouraged to deny our intuition, and when we do this often enough, it shrivels and dies. Yet when we refuse to be governed by intellect alone and listen to this powerful internal voice, our inner power grows and develops.

Intuition is essentially a form of super consciousness, and it finds its path in us via our subconscious. But it's important to understand that the 'I' of our everyday self is the direct opposite of this intuitive state. So put aside your 'I' in order to listen to your intuition.

Through your intuition you can enter a dialogue with the natural world, a communion in which you know and understand the fabric of life. As this happens, your intuitive energy will merge with your inner power, and together they will bring balance, insight and wisdom to you and your world.

16. LIFE'S JOURNEY

All living creatures are part of a whole, called by us the 'cosmos'. We human beings experience ourselves as different and separate from the rest of life, but this is simply an illusion, a kind of misconstruction of our consciousness. This illusion confines and impedes us, keeping us attached to our personal desires and habits.

Our goal must be to free ourselves from the illusion of separateness by enlarging our experience of tolerance, compassion, wisdom, power and generosity to embrace all living creatures and the complete cycle of nature in all its beauty and ugliness. When we are able to do this, we become truly aware and truly alive and we begin to understand our life's journey.

The naturally occurring wisdom of our inner power understands that we are a part of the whole. This deep understanding, evolved from our original experience of being part of all things, shuns dogmas and theology and embraces both the natural and the spiritual.

Life is the transition from birth to death. Death, the next transition, is peaceful if we go through our life's journey being true to ourselves and living as one with the cosmos. When you are connected to your inner power and live in accordance with your own truth, knowing that you are part of the whole of life, connected to every other living creature, you will find the purpose and adventure behind your life's journey.

THE TIBETAN ART OF DREAMING

Sleep gives us a direct link to a more exalted state of consciousness than is normally experienced during the day. Dreaming, according to Tibetan Bön belief, takes place in order that we may stay sane and so that we may expand our consciousness and enable ourselves to connect with our inner power.

Meditation for Making Your Dreams Come True and Developing Your Inner Power

The following steps describe traditional Bön approaches to sleep and dreaming and will enable you to create and influence new and healthy ways of living while you sleep. So not only is this a means to experience profound states of your own inner consciousness but it is also a practical application of your inner power in the everyday world.

Any sleep-related problems should improve with this exercise, as will your overall sense of wellbeing.

STEP ONE: GOING TO BED

Go to bed thirty minutes earlier than normal and lie comfortably on your back. Become aware of the natural cycle of your breath. Merge into your breathing cycle, focusing on it completely. After doing this for at least fifteen minutes, allow your cycle of breathing to slow down. Feel your body becoming heavier and more relaxed, merging into your slow breathing pattern. At this point close your eyes. Now, in your mind's eye, see a gentle, flickering, soft, pink light.

This light slowly grows larger until all that exists is the pink light and your breathing. Rest in the light. Hear the words 'sleep, sleep now' spoken softly to you. The pink light is talking to you. You and the pink light are one. Sleep.

STEP TWO: THE TRANSFORMING SLEEP

As you sleep, call your inner power to you. Allow it to take on a form that you can relate to. This form can be gentle, powerful, stern, wise, playful, animal, vegetable, mineral or human. Allow your inner power to take its time to find its form; you may find that after a few nights of exploration your inner power will settle down and find its form. There is no rush in this part, but you should not go on to step three until your inner power has found its form. When the form is settled, humbly ask it to teach you about the nature of your inner power and its influence upon you, your everyday world, your life, lovers, friends, enemies, family and colleagues.

STEP THREE: PUTTING YOUR INNER POWER TO WORK

After you have learnt about your inner power through dreams, decide upon a course of action that you would like to take at this point in your life. It can be anything that you wish, large or small. This includes self-healing, gaining insight into a situation, ending or beginning a relationship, finding a job or improving your finances.

Now call the form of your inner power out of your mind and describe to it the course of action that you wish to take. After you have done this, see your wish for action growing of its own accord before you, as a clear image. When the image is complete, allow your inner power to breathe life into it. As this happens, state a period in which you wish it to take place. Then be still and give thanks.

STEP FOUR: RECEIVING

Now call forth your inner power and the image of action in your life that you have created and dwell on it from a place of purity and compassion. Fill what you have made with the energy of wisdom, self-creation and benefit to others. As you do this, breathe upon it, filling it with your life force and sending it out into the world. Rest in the pink light. Sleep in your wisdom and illumination.

This meditation can also be used to gain deeper insight into any of the aspects of inner power mentioned in this chapter. Go through the four steps in the same way, simply substituting the aspect of inner power that you are concerned with at step three.

By following this practice regularly, you will develop insight and balance, heal your fears and find serenity, as your inner power grows daily stronger and more confident.

Janice came back from lunch with her friends one Saturday to find that her husband and children had disappeared. Frantically, she called the police, but initially they could tell her nothing.

As she waited for news of her family, Janice discovered that she was also penniless – her bank account had been cleared out and she could not meet the bills or mortgage payments.

After some days Janice learnt that her husband had returned to his homeland in Eastern Europe with her children. Distraught, she decided to fight back. Janice put into effect all practical measures, such as going through the courts, but she was told that she might never win her children back.

At the same time she started to practise the Meditation for Making Your Dreams Come True and Developing Your Inner Power. She was determined that if practical means would not alter her situation, she would do it through her inner power. It took Janice five years to be reunited with her children, but she never gave up hope, and she kept her courage strong through meditation. Eventually, her husband was jailed for kidnapping by the authorities in the country to which he had fled. The children were returned, and Janice remarried and settled down with her family once more.

Today Janice runs a self-help group for teenagers, and she teaches them the Meditation for Making Your Dreams Come True as part of her programme for wellbeing.

5

LOVE

To love and be loved is to feel the warmth of serenity and the absence of fear. Love comes to us to reunite us with life and all its possibilities for a new way of being.

When we love another person, it is the meeting of two energy systems, different from one another, yet at the same time attracted. As love arrives, both are transformed. When both experience love, the emotional and physical nature of each person is changed and raised to a higher level of being. To truly love is to receive a hint of bliss and awakening.

When we love, the happiness of another person becomes essential to our own. Love shows us the bravery of loving without wanting anything in return. Giving because we can. This takes courage, because most of us are scared of falling on our faces and looking silly, or leaving ourselves open to hurt. Yet to go through the process of loving and to follow the call of your heart is an initiation into being truly human. When one human being loves another, the most challenging of all our lessons in life is experienced, that is that each of us can love and none of us is separate from love. Love is the supreme, the ultimate expression of humanity and the path for which all other paths are but preparation.

When we are in love, we have access to wisdom and to becoming wiser. Love gives us, in a blaze, the insight and understanding that would otherwise take years of inner work. Love touches the untouchable and heals that which cannot be healed.

Love is like a beautiful bud, which cannot be forced into blossom, but whose eventual blossoming makes the garden a place of enchantment.

If love is true and real, it is the same whatever or whoever we love, whether that be a person, a belief or a god. Love has no pinnacle or still point; it is like the sea and cannot be measured. It is an act of endless forgiveness and unbreakable tenderness that transforms habits.

And despite the common saying that love is blind, it is in fact not blind at all. Love sees everything, and because it sees all, it is willing and able to see without judgement – it sees things as they are.

Love is more than a feeling. It is essentially a choice to step into accelerated consciousness. If you want to experience love, make the decision to love and to be serene. Do not wait to feel worthy of love, for we cannot do anything that makes us worthy of love, which is simply an offering to us from life. It cannot be earned or given; it exists in all things and can only be recognised and received. Authentic love is a state of communion with all things, and when it happens, there is no need for strategy, control or an outcome.

Yet love does have a strategy, and it is to make sure that eventually every living creature knows love and is supported by it. The greatest contentment of life is the certainty that we are loved for ourselves or, rather, loved regardless of the ways in which we obstruct ourselves.

In this chapter I will take you on a journey through the many aspects of love. Towards the end I will give you a meditation to connect you with the love energy that exists in everything in the world. As you read the chapter, let it become a conversation with your heart. When it feels right to do so, speak the words you are reading out loud. In this way you will enable your heart to open and to unite with love.

When you allow yourself to love, your life will change. When we love, we soften and open. In this enchanted state you will see many aspects of your life differently, making wiser choices and choosing a path of greater serenity.

THE PATH TO LOVE

The greatest thing that each of us will ever achieve is simply to love and be loved in return. It is compassion that brings us the opportunity to love, therefore if you wish to take the path towards love, it is necessary to know the nature of compassion. Compassion is not love, though the two are sometimes confused. Compassion is the absolute kindness of wisdom that knows the essence of all suffering, whereas love is the joy of life, just as it is. The power of compassion transforms fear. To know compassion requires the release of blame, including self-blame. When you release blame, you make a leap of inner trust and your heart opens, allowing you to know your true nature, which loves without fear or insecurity.

In the development of your serenity, gather from yourself all that makes you ill tempered and render it useless until only serenity remains.

Pause for a moment each day and consider this: the truth of love is the truth of the universe. Love is like understanding that grows bright as it gazes on many truths. When, in your experience of loving, you know truth, this same truth is the lamp of the soul that reveals the secrets of fearful darkness.

When you face troubles in life, remember that you are simply being initiated into the mysteries of love. Face your troubles calmly and with love and each and every mystery will reveal itself.

When it comes to the time for us to die, the only thing that we shall be judged on is how we loved and why. When, in the innermost part of your heart, there live words of endless love that are sweet and strong, like the fragrance of rare flowers, you shall pause and know why you are here in this life. In that moment you will know this truth: real love is beyond falling in love with anyone or anything. It is a miracle and capable of creating miracles. Love is that path by which we shall return to our higher selves.

LOVE AND THE SEARCH FOR MEANING

In the search for meaning there are two mistakes you can make. The first is not being prepared to do the necessary work and the second is failing to take the first and most important step: awakening to love.

Nothing will move forward if you do not take these two steps. A person of wisdom lives by doing, not by thinking about doing. Assumptions arrived at through analysis, reason and deliberation have very little influence in altering the course of our lives, whereas actions can move mountains.

In the turbulence of life the most influential actions of our life – those that will decide the whole course of our future – are often unthinking. We are so used to not trusting our inner selves that we allow life to dictate our path. Yet, while this is fine some of the time, in the truly important decisions of life we must take charge. By making the effort to do this, we not only make a conscious choice but we learn how to elevate our consciousness through the choices we make and thereby take full responsibility for them.

Look at every path your life has taken, with scrutiny and with intent, then ask yourself this fundamental question: has this path a spirit? If it has, then the path is skilful and true. If it has not, discard it with compassion and make a new choice. In this way you are doing the necessary work in the search for meaning. The second step, awakening to love, requires us to regard all life and our fellow human beings as equals. This is the humbling action of an awakened human being and takes true self-control to achieve.

Remember that in a world of rage, no person is significant enough to make you angry, if you choose not to be. Learn to move beyond anger to that place in you where everyone is heard. This is the start of a dialogue with love.

THE ROLE OF DEVOTION

The prime energy of love is devotion, which is created from the heart. Devotion is the fire of love and is the essence of how love communicates. It awakens all of you, transforms all resistance of the mind and opens new dimensions of your heart, eventually teaching you the art and power of self-surrender.

Devotion is not a weak or passive energy, nor is it is slavish obedience; it is focused, direct, insightful, questioning and sometimes insistent. It does not tolerate the ranting of fear and insecurity. Devotion teaches us the value of love, for if there is no devotion, there is no love.

Love that becomes fulfilled by devotion and is content unravels mysteries and perceives new meaning and higher reasons behind many of the things that have happened in the past in our lives. With this knowledge you can start to live from your heart.

Living from the heart is the only way of caring for yourself and others. Understanding this, as a species, will take every man, woman and child past the age of information, technology and economics into the age of intuitive living. If we seek to express love by utilising our inherent abilities to serve the world in whatever we do, we find the greatest prospect for our own maturity and that of the world. In this way we give expression to our love for our neighbours and they in turn share that love with others. This is devotion.

LOVE AND FEAR

Fear is what stands in the way of opening our hearts to love. All the ill that is in us comes from fear, and all the good from love. Love is the choice of the brave, who wish to heal their fears.

The fear of love and the serenity created by love are mutually attracted to each other and made by each other. Fear in the face of love tries to puff itself up, making itself more threatening and powerful. When we let our fear blend with our love, as often happens, it creates a painful pollution that derails the path of love and affects the way we receive and experience it. To avoid this, focus solely on increasing the love in your life and leave fear to be on its own, so that it withers, ready for transformation. Let fear find its own path to healing and love its own path to fulfilment.

Remember, when you are most fearful in your experience of love, that there is no antidote for love but to love more. You cannot turn love off; you must let it follow its own course. You must have faith in your love, to know love without having questions, to take a risk. To love in this brave way is to cut your attachments to fear.

When we are wounded in love, it often arouses our fear. Always try to feel affection for the heart that hurts you, and not to wound the heart that loves you. Sometimes this can be the same heart, and in that dwells a paradox: to love makes us vulnerable (and vulnerability can make us afraid), yet it is a blessing to have the courage to trust this vulnerable state. For in this state a great purity and inner clarity is forged – a quality so indestructible that you will always be in the place of love infused with clarity. For in this vulnerability you are always protected by the power of the innocence that comes from this state of consciousness.

When you have finally conquered your fears and healed every vestige of them, then you enter into a state of normality, your fears have gone, life is simple, so in healing fear, you heal your life.

Always remember that there is one thing greater than fear, and that is love. Allow the love within you to conquer your fear.

LOVE AND THOUGHT

In the state of love your thoughts take on new power and influence, so it is important to be careful what you think. See it in this way; your thoughts manifest as words, your words turn to deeds, and often the deed becomes a habit that becomes attached to your character and personality. If the thought, deed and habit is self-defeating or unskilful, then the energy of love within you becomes trapped and the spark of love is lost. So be skilful with your thoughts and how you express them. By this I mean be considerate, and let love permeate and flow through all that you do and say. Let your thoughts, speech and actions be born out of love; for yourself, love for that special person and for all beings.

Love is the prime energy. To have love constantly in your life, let yourself find courage in good thoughts, actions and deeds. Love is not static, unmoving, it constantly reinvents itself, renewing itself, delighting in its own energy. When you can accept this into your consciousness, you will know that love is a gesture from your higher self.

To love is to be given a foretaste of rapture. A rapture that lives, right now, inside you. Face the rapture and gaze into its brilliance.

MEN AND WOMEN

People have long thought that men and women are members of two very different and hostile tribes. In fact, they are not; this is simply a misconception. In truth men and women are the two sides of love seeking itself through human experience.

Underneath the impulse of men and women to be lovers is a restless desire for oneness. There is the continual desire to connect to the wisdom of the human species in one another. This desire is hopeful, natural and an expression of the greater wisdom within us.

However, in today's world many men are confused and ambivalent in their attitudes towards women, wanting a woman who is their equal and yet at the same time fearing such a woman and feeling more at ease with a woman they can dominate. Some men mistrust women or dislike them, because women remind them that they are not as in control as they would like to believe they are. This ambivalence goes back to a lack of understanding of the spiritual nature of man and woman. Fundamental to this is man's relationship with his mother and what she taught him, for the mother, to both men and women, can be seen as the divine source of life, centre of the universe and object of both fear and love. Boys seek the divine unconsciously through their mothers, in an attempt to know it, while girls who, as females, have it within them, seek to be reminded of it. This ancient legacy is an unspoken teaching, the library of the world.

In today's world women are often treated as second best, subject to sexual stereotypes and diminished in the eyes of both men and women. Yet in the ancient Bön tradition it is taught that there can be no spirituality, no sanctity, no emotional evolution of the human race and no truth without the female. The female legacy is the key to the balance and remaking of the fabric of all the life upon this earth, as well as every type of knowledge and event. All things that happen on this planet filter through all women. For women are the regulators of the planet; just as the seasons regulate the earth, so do women. In the same way that some men have misconceptions about women, so some women have misconceptions about men, seeing them as servile creatures who need to be trained and who are inferior to women.

All the misconceptions men and women have about one another come from fear. Let us honour men and honour women, and in that honour chart our fears and receive our serenity. For men and women forget that they are simply love in search of manifestation.

The great wistfulness that exists between the sexes comes from the impermanence of our physical world, the brief span of our lives and the potential enormity of the spiritual that can be experienced within it. Our lives are as a breath caught suddenly, a gasp of surprise, gone, never to be the same again, yet which once expressed becomes one with all other things, seen and unseen. The prime impulse of love is to seek the meaning of life's impermanence through the transformation of fear, and this we men and women seek to do through our connections with one another.

LOOKING FOR LOVE

So many people are searching for love, for that special connection with another person. For most of us, the ultimate goal is to find a companion who, simply by their presence, inspires us to be a better person.

But true love does not enter into our lives when we find the ideal lover – you can look for ever for the perfect person, for they do not exist. All people in the world are flawed, it is the mark of the human condition and true love is found when we become skilled at seeing a flawed person perfectly. How do you do this? By learning to live your life with love.

No amount of honed intellect, creative intelligence or inspired imagination can bring you the experience of love. Love prompts intellect, intelligence and imagination into action, but they cannot reveal the nature of love. To understand the nature of love, it is necessary simply to be loving. Life wants to give you everything that it can, but it can only respond if you express love. What many people need to learn in life is how to love people and make use of things instead of loving things and exploiting people. What matters is not how much or even what you do, but how much love you put into the doing. Everyone you meet, in every station in life, provides you with an opportunity for love. You can find it in an uncomplicated act of kindness toward someone who needs help. You can experience it in a casual conversation or in a moment of warmth from a stranger.

If you grow to be excessively overwhelmed or obsessed

with love, you miss the reality that love can reveal to you. If you calmly and serenely acknowledge love, love will take refuge in your life and talk to you with soft, constant words offering wisdom and comfort. From this point you will be ready to find another human being with whom you will bond deeply and profoundly.

This intimate easiness of love between two human beings cannot be discovered by searching for it or by craving for it. It is spiritual evolution creating divine coincidences. Do not search for love. You already have it.

When you do find love, remember that you cannot look for guarantees. Only fear wants a guarantee, for from the perspective of fear, nothing is strong enough. From the stance of love, none are needed.

Finally, do not forget to love yourself. Love is the sighting of ourselves in others, and without loving yourself it is impossible to love another. Never look to others to make you feel whole, worthwhile or loveable for only you can do that. Be devoted to your own inner consciousness that exists in your heart, mind, speech, deeds and beliefs. By doing this, you become your own person and take charge of yourself.

MARRIAGE

Two people who love each other are in a place more holy than any temple or sacred building, for when we love, the cosmos descends and recreates itself through us. Each of us is formed and created by what we love and what loves us.

Marriage is the blending of two contrasting but essential energies, and so creates expressions of love and the impulse to gain wisdom. This is nothing less than the very serenity that unites the cosmos.

By marriage I mean the coming together of two people, not necessarily in a formal union, but in mutual commitment. In the Bön tradition the act of sexual intercourse is in itself designated marriage. This is because during intercourse people take on the energy of one another.

Couples absorb the minds and the bodies of each other into their own energy systems; they evolve a new version of the other while remaking themselves as they unite together. That is what marriage is a symbol of, because we take on the deepest part of our partners, the energy of each combines to make a new creation, a new way of living; that is, the relationship. A wonderful marriage is not when the perfect people meet each other and join together, it is when an imperfect couple learns to enjoy their differences in a spirit of love, and from this point, help one another to become better people. In a good marriage the rest of the world is not excluded. Love does not consist of gazing at each other but in mutually looking outward in the same stream of awareness.

When you look at marriage, you experience creation itself. Marriage is as important an experience as birth and death. It links people to the past and guides them to an unknown future, thus establishing a sense of continuity.

All married couples should learn the skills of making love, emotionally, spiritually and physically, as well as the path of skilful and loving combat, which is the ability to have a constructive argument. Skilful combat is impartial and straightforward – never brutal or spiteful. Skilful combat is good for your health and productive, bringing to a marriage the faith in each other that comes from a dynamic understanding.

WHEN LOVE GOES WRONG

When love goes wrong, people blame themselves, or the world, or the other person and sometimes all three. Yet love does not in fact go wrong; it merely changes its flow. Love is a powerful force that needs a strong container to hold its energy. It will find the most direct path it can, but if the structures are not in place, then it moves on to find a more enduring connection.

All unequal partnerships have to become balanced or they disintegrate. The simplest key to creating this balance is for both people in a relationship to try to live day by day helping each other, being good to themselves and being good to each other.

Love will also go wrong when we neglect the opportunity to love ourselves. Do not make the mistake of looking to another person to make you feel loveable or worthwhile. This is your responsibility. If you come to a relationship with a strong sense of self and of the qualities you have, then you come to it ready to give and receive love.

In long relationships people sometimes confuse comfort and habit with love. Each of these has its place, but what they offer are not the same. Love brings risk and transformation; habit and comfort create a smaller world, one that is easier to control.

To love means to be vulnerable to the negative and the positive – to heartache, unhappiness and disillusionment, as well as to bliss, serenity and an expansion of consciousness we did not know was possible before. Hate is not the reverse of love, indifference is, and fear is at the heart of indifference. Courage is born from love, and without courage, our love fades into habit or allows indifference to become dominant.

Jealousy is often seen as linked to love, yet jealousy is a

disease while love is a healthy condition. The immature mind often mistakes one for the other, or assumes that the greater the love, the greater the jealousy. In fact, they are almost incompatible; jealousy hardly leaves room for love. The love that makes demands is, in reality, fear. When you are able to love and make no demands, this is the truest intimation of your highest enlightenment.

When two people part, it can feel like a terrible separation, ripping them apart. Yet this is because we regard love in a limited and fearful way, attaching ourselves to the concepts of beginnings and endings. Genuine love goes on for ever. Grief, tragedy and hatred are only temporary. Goodness, remembrance and love have no end.

Meditation for Healing the End of a Relationship

If you know that your relationship has come to an end, you will find this meditation helpful. Practise it as often as you wish.

Close your eyes, see your ex partner in your mind, naked. Now see a clear white light coming from above and flooding over them. They dissolve into the light, and as they do, so do the parts of you in them, and those parts of them in you. Any emotional garbage evaporates, and you are left with lessons that enrich your life. Give thanks and be silent for as long as you can.

THE SIGNIFICANCE OF LOVE

Love enriches the soul, brings gladness to the heart and affirms that life is sacred.

In my work, giving lectures and seminars around the world as well as in my London clinic, I have never met a person whose utmost desire was anything other than sincere, unlimited love.

Consider this – if you learnt that you had only moments left to live, what would you wish to express to the people you are closest to? The answer for all of us, I believe, is love.

There is no confusion with love. You experience it in your heart as the shared filament of life, the glow that brings pure ardour into our soul, supports our spirit and contributes understanding and tolerance to our lives. It is our connection to spirituality and holiness and our most powerful connection to one another. In order to create anything of value in your life, there needs to be a vibrant delight, and what delight is more compelling than love? In times of doubt in your life, be patient about all that is puzzling your heart. There are times in life when you have more questions than answers. In order to find the right answers, you need to love the questions themselves. Pour love on them until they melt. Love also offers us the key to freedom. To be free is not to cast off one's restraints but to live in a way that respects, inspires and increases the freedom of others – in other words, to live a loving life. To do this, never accept an evil that you can change and in all that you do in life, let love be its motivation. Treat everything and everyone with love – whether it be triumph, disaster, friend, enemy, problem or joy.

Meditation on Love

This meditation will help you connect to the love energy that exists in all things and all people in the world. It will enable you to enhance all your experiences of love, and it will connect you to the deeper spiritual love that lives within us all.

It will also help to bring a special person into your life, if that is what you are seeking.

The meditation is very simple and very powerful. Therefore I suggest that you do it in stages.

Firstly, do it over a nine-day period, so that you are used to it, then progress to an eighteen-day period. From that you can move on to a twenty-seven-day period. Leave nine days between each of these time periods.

In each of these cycles I suggest that you do the meditation at the same time each day. The best times of day are 5 a.m. to 10 a.m. and then in the twilight hours of 4 p.m. until 7 p.m. In addition the hours of 11 p.m. until 1 a.m. are good.

Close your eyes.

Give thanks for all the heartbreaks, hurts and difficulties in your life connected to love.

Give thanks for all the uplifting and happy moments love has brought you.

Then give thanks that you are able to give thanks.

Now be as still as you can. Be aware of the space around you and of the heartbeat within you. Concentrate on your heartbeat, and with each beat of your heart see your body and your mind beginning to shine. Now see a light coming out of your body. As the light starts to become bright, turning from pearl white to transparent, it starts to sing, beginning with one clear, bell-like voice and progressing to a thousand bell-like voices.

Listen closely, hear the song and then the words. Know that for each of us the melody, harmony and tune within the song are the same, but the words are different, bringing us a unique message. As you listen to the words, you will hear your own special message.

As you listen, start to sing along with the words, burning them into your soul. When you feel ready to stop, allow the song to merge with the world around you. Breathe in and then out slowly, and then clap your hands together with intent and force to energetically close the meditation and bring it into focus.

This meditation is simple yet full of revelation. Each time you perform it, the words will be the same until such time as you have learnt the lesson that your soul is teaching you. When you are ready for the next step, the words will change but not the song itself.

Lorna's marriage came crashing down around her, and after a gruesome divorce, she was alone and felt shattered and completely broken. She felt she had lost the love of her life in her husband, and as he moved on to a new relationship, she became sick.

As her illness became worse, her loss became more intense. When she came to see me, Lorna had developed the symptoms of ME, she was constantly ill and exhausted and she felt her life was not worth living.

I asked Lorna to practise the Meditation on Love and, at the same time, to focus her energy on looking after herself in a loving and nurturing way.

After the first nine-day period of the meditation, Lorna felt a shift in her energy. After the eighteen-day period of meditating, she was well enough to ride her horse, something she had not done for a year. After the twenty-seven-day period of meditation, she felt strong enough to pack up her husband's possessions and send them to him, with a warm note wishing him well.

From this point Lorna moved on to good health and, within a year, a new relationship. Her joy in life had returned and she was able to see the blessings she and her husband had brought one another in their five years together.

Terence had everything in life but love. He was well off and had an exciting job as a news reporter, but his love life was a disaster. As he went from one failed relationship to another, he felt more and more downcast. He longed for a settled relationship and for children, but the women he attracted were not interested in permanence.

Terence began the Meditation on Love and soon realised that he was chasing love much too hard and that he must let it come to him. He concentrated his energy on feeling loveable and on being calm, relaxed and accepting. For six months he didn't ask anyone out or do any chasing, he simply allowed himself to believe that when the time was right, love would come to him.

One day a woman Terence had known for some time as a friend told him that she had fallen in love with him. He was amazed and delighted to find that he felt deeply for her too. Within a year they were married, and six years on they have two children and are extremely happy.

6

LONELINESS

Every one of us feels lonely at some point in our life. It is part of the human condition to experience, at times, a sense of isolation from others, regardless of whether others are present or not.

For those people for whom loneliness is a transitory and brief state, it is simply something to accept and understand. But for others, loneliness is not a passing phase but a way of life that comes to feel like a trap from which they cannot escape, and when this happens, there is often great suffering.

Loneliness is not the same as being alone. It is quite possible to be alone and to feel content, fulfilled and at peace. In this state solitude can be a joy and a blessing, allowing the individual time and space to explore their own inner life, to experience tranquillity and to spend time with themselves in a loving way. In a state of solitude you feel connected to others, even if they are not present. Solitude is without fear or distress and is a peaceful state.

Loneliness, on the other hand, is unhappiness at being alone and is experienced as a state of separation from the rest of the world and an inability to communicate with others and thereby awaken our connections to them. When we are lonely, we feel an inner sense of emptiness, helpless in our isolation and closed off from life.

There are different forms of loneliness. You might experience it as vague, unformed emotions that tell you something is not right, a kind of fleeting void. Alternatively, you might feel loneliness as a very intense withdrawal, like an acute pain or a constant dull ache.

Loneliness also has many superficial causes. It might be that you are missing someone who has died or from whom you are separated. It might be that you are living or working alone and have little contact with others. Or it might be that you are around others, even in a relationship, but simply feel disconnected, unheard and unable to reach out for contact and support.

What all loneliness has in common is the pattern it creates in us of building walls instead of bridges. The more lonely someone feels, the more they cut themselves off from others and the harder it feels to imagine making a real and meaningful connection with another person.

All loneliness also has in common the same source – fear. And in our modern world fear, and therefore loneliness, is growing. Many of us now live in societies, particularly in the West, in which more and more people feel isolated and disconnected from how they feel and how those feelings affect the world. This sense of disconnection breeds fear, which in turn breeds loneliness. The tragedy of this is that no one need feel lonely. Like all other conditions, loneliness is simply a state of mind. The difference between joyous solitude and sorrowful loneliness is within each one of us. And if we are willing, we can learn how to heal the sorrow of loneliness and turn its bitterness into the sweetness of inner peace and the ability to choose either solitude or the meaningful company of others.

Like all human conditions, loneliness has within it great blessings, if we are willing to see them. By exploring your loneliness, you will discover a sense of purpose about your life, what it is you want to do and to live for. You will also discover the serenity within you, along with the ability you have to think, create and interact with other people.

In this chapter I will explain in more depth what loneliness is and what its causes are. I will go on to show you how to bless and then dissolve your loneliness, discover instead the joy of solitude and of connecting with others in a fulfilling way.

❖

MISUNDERSTANDING LONELINESS

Loneliness can be made more intense by the way you talk to yourself about it. There are misconceptions about loneliness, which many people believe and repeat to themselves, reinforcing their unhappy messages. These include the belief that loneliness is a sign of weakness or immaturity or that there's something 'wrong' with you if you are lonely.

Many people believe that no one else feels the way they do, that everyone else is out in the world enjoying great relationships and effortless contact with others. Needless to say, none of these misconceptions is true. But if you believe any of them, then you may feel that your loneliness results from a defect in your personality. And when you allow yourself to believe this, it can lead to problems which include:

- A greater fear of taking social risks, such as making phone calls to initiate social contact, introducing yourself to others, participating in groups of any kind, from reading circles to parties.
- A lessening in self-expression and responsiveness to others.
- A greater tendency to approach social encounters with cynicism and mistrust.

- An increased likelihood of evaluating yourself and others in negative terms.
- A greater expectation that others will reject you.

Lonely people often tell me that they are feeling depressed, angry, afraid and misunderstood. Many are highly critical of themselves, overly sensitive or self-pitying, and they are often critical and blaming of others too. The result of this is that lonely people often begin doing things that perpetuate their loneliness. Some, for example, become discouraged, losing the impetus to get involved in new situations, and isolating themselves from people and activities. Others deal with loneliness by becoming involved too quickly and deeply with people or activities, without evaluating the consequences of their involvement. They may later find themselves in unsatisfying relationships or over-committed to work, religious beliefs or study.

The alternative to viewing loneliness as something bad, a defect or an unalterable personality characteristic is to recognise that it is common to many people in all sectors of society and that, far from being 'set in stone', it can be transformed into an entirely different experience. Loneliness is simply a signal that important needs are going unmet and that action is needed.

SORROW

Sorrow is the emotion that keeps you addicted to loneliness. Loneliness often comes from a deep, abiding sorrow that lies within you. It can come from unhappy relationships or because you are not doing what you love or living as you should. It can emanate from the very nature of existence, life and people. Sometimes the world can be a very overwhelming place, and its sheer power can cause us to retreat from life.

The more entrenched we become in retreat, the more we believe that the only way to cope with life is to escape from reality. If we have this type of sorrow, then unfortunately we create a grim existence for ourselves through our fears. But even if you are in the grip of a powerful sorrow, you can still alter your experience of loneliness. Inside all of us is a place where we live all alone and where we renew our inner selves. In this place you create inspired thoughts that lead you to self-discovery. It is a place free from sorrow and from fear, and when we have access to it, we can choose not to be lonely.

THE WEST'S INHERITANCE OF LONELINESS

Loneliness is prevalent in today's developed Western societies for a number of reasons.

In the West most people live in built-up and populated communities where they are physically close to each other yet emotionally very detached from each other. Close proximity does not necessarily translate into close relationships or communities and the result is what I think of as 'crowded loneliness'.

People are also working more and therefore connecting less in a social and community sense. When twenty-four-hour industrial plants and offices dominate an area's economy, neighbours remain strangers. Those who work long hours tend to lead lonelier and less satisfying lives.

Loneliness is one of the results of the accelerating fragmentation of the family and the steady rise in the number of broken families. In addition, in many areas the older population is separated from the younger and this increases social fears and social illness.

Another reason for social isolation is the predominant desire for privacy. Privacy is a modern invention that has come to be considered indispensable and even a status symbol in many communities. But with privacy comes distance, and those who seal themselves away from others behind walls and alarms often reduce the possibility of warm and neighbourly contact.

What is valued in today's societies is mobility, privacy and convenience, all of which have the potential to increase isolation and loneliness and make developing a sense of community almost impossible.

In earlier periods of human history, when extended families made up most of the community, the idea of adults living alone and prizing privacy above contact was unimaginable. Yet now many adults, particularly the youngest and oldest but often those in between as well, live alone for long periods of time. The young are delaying entering into permanent relationships or marriage, so extending the number of years of being single. The search for material success, personal identity and fulfilment are most often behind the choice to stay single for longer and increasing numbers of adults are living most or all of their lives alone. Today in the Western world one in every four households contains just one person. If the current trends continue, this proportion will soon increase to one in every three households for the rest of the twenty-first century. The twentieth century was the century of violence; the twenty-first will become the century of loneliness.

Not only is this generation marrying less and marrying later, they also stay married less than their parents. The current generation has the highest divorce rate of any generation in history. And not only do they divorce more often, they divorce earlier. When the divorce rate shot up in the sixties and seventies, the increase was not due to empty nesters filing for divorce after sending their children into the world, it was due to young couples divorcing before they even had children. The result is that more and more middle-aged adults find themselves living alone.

While the increase in adults living alone is unprecedented, many others are living in relationships that leave them feeling very much alone. The increase in sexual freedom and the choice of lifestyle opportunities means that many adults may be less committed to making marriage work than in previous generations. Relationships, which are ideally the source of stability and intimacy, often produce uncertainty and isolation, and people who are unskilfully bound in a relationship may be lonelier than a person living alone.

The changing roles of men and women have also created a turbulent crisis of expectations. In the last few decades the expectations that men have of women and that women have of men have changed for ever. When these expectations do not match reality, disappointment and loneliness sets in.

Increasingly, when I talk to those who come to see me, whatever their initial problems, I come across the following responses, all of which only serve to increase a sense of loneliness. People tell me they:

- Cannot turn to each other when they feel down.
- Are left out of each other's lives.
- Feel isolated from each other, even when they are in the same room.
- Become unhappy being shut off from each other.
- Feel that no one really knows them well.

These five expressions indicate that loneliness has become a social belief and a widespread state of mind.

LONELINESS AND THE CHRISTIAN LEGACY

In the Christian tradition that has so influenced the West the teachings of Christ have supported loneliness, creating a legacy of cultural sorrow. It is evident that Jesus experienced loneliness. When he said, 'I was hungry and you fed me,' he did not mean simply hunger for food but also hunger for love. Jesus lived among his own people as a teacher, and they did not want anything to do with him. It hurt him emotionally and spiritually, and it has kept on hurting, in the beliefs and actions supported by the dogma of his followers. This hunger, the same loneliness, the having of no one to be accepted by and to be loved and wanted by, is a malady of the modern world as transmitted into people's consciousness by Christianity of all types.

According to the unconscious inheritance of Christianity, every human being resembles Jesus, the spiritual teacher, in his loneliness. This is the legacy inherited by the West, etched by religion and underpinned by popular culture.

MEN AND LONELINESS

It is through men that fear has found the most successful path to loneliness. Women are more likely than men to express their emotions and display understanding in response to the emotional needs of others. Men, on the other hand, are frequently isolated by the force of their fear and therefore have fewer truly close friends.

The following seven unskilful qualities of loneliness are to be found woven tightly into men's legacy in the modern world. All of these become barriers to friendship and intimacy and are created by our fears and our lack of serenity.

1. Men feel discomfort at letting others see their emotions. Expressing feelings has become a fearful passage for males. At a young age boys receive the cultural instruction that they must be strong and enduring, and as a result, as men, they shirk their emotional responsibilities. Such an aversion makes deep relationships difficult, so men find it difficult to make and keep friendships, for they have not been taught the truth that manliness comes from humanity.

2. Men have created a block to true companionship. Men may get together collectively for commercial activities, amusement or leisure, but they seldom do so just to enjoy each other's company and to find real comradeship.

3. Men have learnt to create and pass on poor emotional and spiritual examples. The tough guy's disguise of aggressiveness and strength keeps men from knowing themselves and others.

4. The powerful influence of male rivalry means that men feel they must excel in whatever they do, in order to be someone or something. This is a false assumption and the competitive spirit it encourages is frequently a barrier to friendship.

5. Men rarely ask for help because they see it as a sign of weakness. Unskilful male attempts at self-sufficiency rob them of fulfilling relationships.

6. Success and status for many men is determined by material wealth rather than by the quality of close friendships they have. Men tend to restrict their friendships and thus their own identity.

7. Men often focus on one aspect of life, such as career, to the detriment of others. When this happens it becomes far more likely that a man will experience a personal crisis. Many men today have a limited sense of identity, and this makes them fragile. Men need to expand their sense of identity by seeing themselves in many roles rather than one or two.

TRANSFORMING LONELINESS

Loneliness is a submissive state, and when we passively accept it, we maintain it. The fear behind loneliness wants everything to stay the same, and this fear prevents us from taking action. We hope the loneliness will go away yet allow it to choke us.

Accepting loneliness and the unhappy experiences associated with it leads to dejection and defencelessness, which then creates even greater passivity. To transform loneliness, it is necessary to take action. Loneliness is not pointless or a waste of time. Far from it – in Tibetan Bön culture loneliness is one of the necessary experiences we must go through in order to discover our true potential and to grow in inner strength and wisdom. We all have within us, waiting to be discovered, an inner fire, which is able to consume loneliness and the fear behind it, revealing the maturing soul. And the reason so many people, all over the world, are enduring the painful lessons of loneliness is that we are moving towards a new dimension in consciousness. This will emerge as people the world over discover the joy of transforming loneliness into serenity and joy. Here are the first three steps towards transforming loneliness:

- Spend a short period, of say fifteen minutes, in silence each morning. You will soon discover that a few minutes of conscious silence will ease months of loneliness.
- In addition, spend a little time each day looking within and discovering the origins of your loneliness. Do not be afraid to embrace the sorrow that your fears have created and the habits that you have made to keep the world at a distance. The daily observing and under-standing of your fears changes them. When you are willing to open yourself to the pain that they hold, they will begin to transform into love and loneliness will lose its grip on you.
- Express yourself by writing a journal, painting, composing or in some other creative way. Bringing out the emotional energy inside you in this way will reveal and release the feelings behind your loneliness.

Practical Solutions

Sometimes it is necessary to pursue practical solutions to loneliness alongside the spiritual path. Loneliness is often dissolved by learning ways of becoming more self-sufficient and of reaching out to others.

When you are willing to reach out in friendship, it will immediately increase your energy, happiness and self-confidence.

Here are eight ways of making friendships, one or more of which may be valuable in breaking through your sense of loneliness:

1. Look for ways, every day, to get involved with people. Make conversation when the opportunity arises and extend warmth to a stranger.

2. Put yourself in new situations where you will meet people, perhaps through activities in which you have genuine interest, or through offering help and support to others.

3. Learn from others. When you see someone who is good at connecting with others and making friends, take instruction from them, whether through observation or by asking them for ideas.

4. Strengthen your social skills by smiling, talking and engaging with others whenever possible.

5. Try to see each person you meet from a new perspective, rather than pre-judging them.

6. Avoid rushing into intimate friendships by sharing too quickly or expecting that others will. Let the process develop naturally.

7. Value all of your friendships and their unique characteristics rather than believing that only a romantic relationship will relieve your loneliness.

8. Be prepared to extend trust without seeking anything in return.

CREATING SELF-LOVE

The unconscious mission of people everywhere is to escape the loneliness that they sense as they lose touch with the sacred soul energy of life. Yet the answer is not to escape loneliness but rather to embrace it by learning self-love. For you shall not be lonely if you are fond of the person you are alone with. Learn to love yourself and loneliness simply does not exist. The Tibetan Bön tradition suggests that self-love is the first essential step to being able to take charge of your life and to make a life that is rewarding.

The creation of self-love also brings the confidence that helps you to open yourself to the world and to identify and connect with others. This aspect is important, for self-love with no regard for others is simply fear in another guise and will lead to the greatest loneliness of all.

At the core of all human loneliness is an intense and compelling craving for a coming together with one's lost self. We enter the world alone and we leave the world alone, but we do not enter the world in loneliness. At the beginning of life we are at peace with ourselves, connected and complete. Sadly, many people come to believe, over the years, that they are separate from their inner selves. The sense of inner connection disappears as fear takes a grip.

The truth is that none of us are separate from our inner selves; we simply become confused. As confusion clears we once again feel connected to ourselves, to life, love, serenity and to other people.

Self-love is the heart of all inner value and balance. You can develop it by knowing how you live and the value of your life and its influence upon other people. Self-love drives out all feelings of separation and loneliness and connects you to everything; it encourages other people to love you and to want to be with you. Here is a meditation on self-love. I suggest that you do it at least once a day for ten minutes.

Meditation on Self-love

Sit quietly and close your eyes. See your body dissolve into a pile of ash and then see it remake itself. All your emotions and negativities from the past dissolve and you are filled with calmness, quiet and rest.

In developing self-love, it is important not to concentrate on the spiritual alone but also to include practical self-care. Loving concern for yourself is a vital part of self-love and will support your spiritual development. Make sure that you eat well, take exercise and get enough sleep. And feed your spirit by doing things that you enjoy, such as listening to music, reading poetry or walking in beautiful surroundings.

Never define yourself as a lonely person. Loneliness will diminish when you focus attention and energy on the needs you have which you can meet yourself. Do not wait for your feelings to get you going – get going and good feelings will catch up with you.

Sam found it hard to connect with other people. His one serious girlfriend had left him, after two years together, when he was twenty-two, and he became shy and withdrawn as a result. When I met Sam, he was twenty-eight and very lonely. He worked as a decorator, mostly on his own, and lived alone in a small flat. His home was scruffy and uncared for and so was he. Sam had no idea how to look after himself and no confidence in his ability to interest or attract friends and prospective partners.

Sam came to me because he had a bad back, but it was immediately clear that his back problem was the superficial aspect of his life problem, which was loneliness.

While treating Sam's back, I also asked him to practise the Meditation on Self-love daily. He was surprised, but as a sensitive and intelligent young man, he immediately recognised that it might help him. I suggested that Sam put some effort into self-care, making sure that he ate healthily, got plenty of sleep, looked after his appearance and made a pleasant home for himself.

Over the next few months Sam's back improved and so did his general appearance. He arrived for his appointments looking smart and clean and told me that he had decorated his flat, bought himself some new clothes, given up smoking and improved his diet.

On his last visit to me Sam told me that he was dating a girl he had met in his local supermarket. He'd found the confidence to start talking to her and they immediately found they had a lot in common. For Sam, self-care was the route out of his loneliness.

THE FOUR SORROWS OF LONELINESS

In the Tibetan Bön tradition it is said that loneliness is made of four sorrows. They are listed below. Read each of them aloud, and as you do this, weigh and consider each sentence. This is a form of meditation, and as you speak, it will awaken answers within you and you will see how each of the sorrows has influenced your life. You will notice the instructions for different breath patterns preceding and following each sorrow. This is designed to increase your inner perceptions.

Write down the feelings and answers that come to you after each point is spoken aloud. Do this daily for at least twelve days. Then consider all your answers and how they reflect and reveal your inner self to you.

Practising this meditation will heal your loneliness and help you to be at peace and find contentment within yourself.

Meditation on the Four Sorrows of Loneliness

Each breath in and out is counted as one cycle.

(Breathe in and out slowly nine times and then speak the first sentence.)
One: The sorrow of loneliness from unhappy relationships.
(Breathe in and out slowly nine times and consider what it means.)

(Breathe in and out slowly seven times and then speak the second sentence.)
Two: The sorrow of loneliness that comes from not doing what you love.
(Breathe in and out slowly seven times and consider what it means.)

(Breathe in and out slowly five times and then speak the third sentence.)
Three: The sorrow of loneliness that comes from not living as you should.
(Breathe in and out slowly five times and consider what it means.)

(Breathe in and out slowly three times and then speak the fourth sentence.)
Four: The sorrow of loneliness that emanates from the very nature of existence.
(Breathe in and out slowly three times and consider what it means.)

Each one of us, during our lifetime, will have had some experience of these four sorrows. But by knowing that loneliness is not a lasting condition, you can move beyond it.

Love and serenity dissolve all loneliness, for loneliness is a fearful and unskilful connection to the world around us. Take time each day to be still and to find your heart and then dwell upon the serenity that is within you.

Life is sacred, and we are all connected to each other and responsible for each other's wellbeing. With each day we can come closer to knowing ourselves through the experiences of other people, for we are not separate but are part of the human family.

Julia was a successful doctor who had lived alone since her last relationship ended five years earlier. At fifty-five she was comfortably off, owned a lovely home and had three cats she adored. She found her work very satisfying and had no real desire for another relationship. However, Julia felt lonely and longed to feel more comfortable and at peace in her own company. She wasn't interested in joining clubs; she had never felt comfortable in groups. She had a handful of good friends who were important to her, but they couldn't fill the void she felt when she was alone.

'How do I become happier in my own company?' she asked me. She admitted that she was highly self-critical and felt she must be at fault because she was lonely.

I asked Julia to suspend her self-criticism and think instead about the fact that she chose to live alone and had a very good life. In addition, I asked her to practise the Meditation on the Four Sorrows of Loneliness daily for twelve days and see what it brought for her.

When Julia came back to see me, she said she had realised, after doing the meditation, that her loneliness stemmed back to her childhood. She had always been a solitary child, but her father had been very critical of this and told her repeatedly that she should seek out the company of others. Once she realised this, Julia was able to let go of her self-criticisms and to begin to enjoy her own company, something she had naturally done as a child.

7

FEELING OVERWHELMED

Have you ever rushed around a room searching your pockets, anxiously rummaging for your keys? Or walked into a room and forgotten why you went in there? Or forgotten a word that was on the tip of your tongue? Have you ever had a sudden bout of fatigue or experienced bizarre shifts in time? Have you had moments when you questioned what was going on with your short-term memory?

It is likely that you will have answered yes to at least one of these questions. And not surprising, because all of the above behaviours are signs of overwhelm, and we live in an age when, for most people, overwhelm is normal.

The amount of information we are expected to absorb in any given day is many many times what our ancestors, even those a generation or two back, had to deal with. We are confronted by television, radio, internet, telephones, newspapers, multiple demands, complex daily routines and endless noise. And all this on far less sleep than previous generations had.

Little wonder, then, that overwhelm is a major issue in our world today. Our brains are struggling to cope and adapt to the avalanche of information thrown at them, and of course this takes time – more time than we have in our lifetimes. When the brain can't cope, it switches off. Many of us spend a lot of our time in a state of dissociation from our surroundings because it's the only way we can cope. Breakdowns, depression and mental illness are all vastly on the increase. We don't know how to protect ourselves from the overwhelm we face, and illness is often the consequence.

Tragically, being overwhelmed is now accepted as part of daily living. We expect it and we treat it as normal. But overwhelm is not normal, it is an unnatural state, a state of fear and disconnection, which is threatening to our health and wellbeing. When we are overwhelmed, we are no longer connected to the life-giving forces of the natural world. Instead, we are in the grip of a build-up of fear – the chattering fear caused by worry, anxiety and confusion. As this happens, we pull back – retreat is the automatic response to overwhelm. We pull our fragile consciousness back from the world, and this results in disconnection, not only from what hurts us but from all that is good and life-enhancing.

Many people are so overwhelmed by demands for their focus, concentration, memory, time and attention that they switch off and live their lives in a kind of stunned trance. You can often observe this on the faces of people around you – or when you look in the mirror.

Overwhelm drugs the ability to be truly perceptive about yourself and about the world around you. It dramatically reduces the quality of your life. Taken to an extreme, fanaticism, extremism and terrorism of any type come from the helplessness of being overwhelmed.

We live in an age where we have outstripped our own ability to cope. We have invented machines and technologies that make demands our brains and bodies cannot deal with. When this happens, technology becomes a channel for anxiety and fear. We have made a tool of global change and yet we do not understand its long-term effects upon the individual psyche or that of the planet.

We have learnt to react to technology but not to understand when the brain is overwhelmed. Many people reach a point where they fail to notice the signs of overwhelm and simply treat tiredness, memory loss, illness and so on as normal. We feel helpless in the face of continual overwhelm, and yet it is entirely possible to live a life free from overwhelm. If you are willing, you can create new attitudes and learn new skills that will allow you to avoid overwhelm and make wiser, clearer choices about your life. Avoiding technology is not an option – unless you want to go and live at the top of a mountain somewhere. But living with it in such a way that you use and control it while preventing it from overwhelming you is absolutely possible. The modern world is filled with desperate and unskilful influences, but you can choose to maintain emotional and mental independence, no matter what.

THE FOUR STEPS TO CLARITY

The antidote to overwhelm is clarity. If your mind is clear, you can think, make decisions, judge what is best and put your focus where it is needed. With clarity comes increased ability, whereas when we are overwhelmed, all abilities are reduced; we hear, think, speak and see less well. Overwhelm saps our life force, keeping us in a shadow existence, whereas clarity strengthens and rejoices in the life force.

In the Bön tradition there are four steps necessary to dislodge the state of overwhelm and increase clarity. Work through the steps one by one. As you do, you will enable yourself to move overwhelm towards the brilliant light and transcendent consciousness of clarity.

STEP ONE

Determine your priorities and focus on them.

This is the most difficult of the four steps, so spend ten minutes at the start of your day focusing on it, in order to make it part of your life.

Don't let yourself be pulled towards anything – from business meetings to casual conversations – that feels time wasting. Instead, make space in your day for the things that are important to you: from projects, to exercise, to family time. Hold these times as sacred.

STEP TWO

Revolutionise the way you communicate.

Closely examine the way you speak and look at what is behind your words, for speech is emotion, thought, action and deed. Therefore speak carefully and with respect in everything.

Learn to speak from your heart. By this I mean don't talk about what is wrong but concentrate instead on what is right. Don't complain, belittle others or predict disaster. Instead, use your speech to praise, appreciate and be optimistic. Let your speech be a starting point of harmony and a tool to disentangle the confusion that creates the state of being overwhelmed.

STEP THREE

Change the way you work.

Does your work contain the passion of your self? If not, reclaim your life. If your work is making you sick, bitter or no longer reflects the way you are, release it, for it is a contagious disease, which will be affecting the whole of your life.

Choose instead to find work that supports who you are and your dreams, hopes and abilities. Too often we are hostage to work, believing that we must do jobs we hate in order to earn money. Have the courage to leave behind this way of thinking and the support you need will come to you.

STEP FOUR

Create calm.

To find a sense of inner calm, take five minutes a day to practise paying attention to just one thing. This may be anything – your breathing, a flower, an object, even a traffic light. It doesn't matter what it is, what matters is that you observe the divine within it.

Like the muscles in our bodies, the brain becomes stronger as we train it. And this focusing exercise trains the brain to recognise and accept calm. The calmer you are, the less overwhelmed you become, for from calmness comes the path to serenity.

Focusing on just one thing starts to awaken your inner consciousness and allows you to recognise that the ability to meditate is naturally within you and not something you have to acquire or do.

Single-pointed focus stabs fear to the core, while drawing out the serenity within you to the point where it spills like a flood out into your everyday mind, imbuing all things with wellbeing.

FREEDOM FROM OVERWHELM

Freeing yourself from overwhelm is a challenge. Many people think a challenge is too daunting; they reject something that may be difficult, preferring to live with whatever is unpleasant in their lives. But to meet a challenge is a wonderful thing. A challenge presents us with the opportunity to prove our power to ourselves and to others. To be delighted with life and to live with joy, you must accept all challenges that come your way.

In meeting the challenge of overwhelm, there are a number of ways forward that you must follow:

KNOW YOUR OWN TRUTH

By this I mean follow your heart and not the dictates of others. Other people want you to believe in and take on their opinions and their truths. We are bombarded with the opinions of others, from advertisers to politicians, to those of different religions, to friends and partners. But while you may listen politely to others and keep an open mind, you must know your own truth.

To truly overcome the feelings of being overwhelmed, activate your desire for self-knowledge. By doing this sincerely, everything else falls into place. Trust your path as it shows itself to you and from this act of trust you will know how to move forward. The more you trust yourself and follow what you know to be your truth, the stronger and clearer you will be.

As you gain self-knowledge, others around you may want you to stay overwhelmed, in order to maintain things just as they are. Some may get sad, others angry. They may feel displaced by you as the trappings of your fear of overwhelm fall away. Acknowledge the feelings of others, but don't sway your truth in order to rescue others from their discomfort.

KNOW YOUR OWN VALUE

Never be caught up in the fear that you are not of value. When people do this, they look for a measure of their value in others or in their achievements. Many people, especially in the West, measure their value by what they own or what they earn. This is a great mistake and leads directly to overwhelm, for then they feel that they can only increase their value by owning or earning more. Yet such a sense of value is worthless and ineffectual. Your true sense of value can only come from within and is not connected to a job, a possession or another person. It comes from the knowledge that as a living being, you have value.

REJECT TOXIC THOUGHTS

The most contagious part of overwhelm is the toxic shock that comes from toxic thinking and the dark world that this makes. If you think about troubles, they grow bigger. To stop being overwhelmed, you need to change your thinking patterns, and the content and quality of your thoughts.

Making optimism a way of life restores your faith in yourself and rejects overwhelm, so make a conscious daily effort to replace unhappy, unkind and doubtful thoughts with thoughts filled with life energy and belief in all that is good. Forgive those who hurt you and release yourself from the pain of bitterness. Choose faith in the good in the world over doubt and fear.

DO NOT BE DISCOURAGED

Every unskilful effort thrown to the wind is one more fortunate step forward. The higher your state of inner energy when life is bringing you challenges, the better you deal with them.

And as you resolve them, you move further from the influences of all that is overwhelming in the world. It is as if you have walked from out of a misty valley to a high mountain top from where you can look down to the next valley and from your vantage point know the nature of the next step of your journey.

MAKE EVERY OBSTRUCTION AN OPPORTUNITY FOR SELF-KNOWLEDGE

The energies of the earth and the universe will not give you anything that you cannot deal with. This is at the heart of self-knowledge.

Self-knowledge is not what happens to a person. It is what a person does with what happens to them in life. Small and fragile minds are restrained and intimidated by misfortune, but empowered minds rise above it and face adversity with courage. The greater your self-knowledge, the more you will be able to overcome obstructions in your life.

CREATE SPACE FOR STILLNESS

In twenty-first-century society the noise level is such that it keeps knocking our bodies out of tune and out of their natural rhythms. This ever-increasing assault of sound upon our ears, minds and bodies adds greatly to our overwhelm, as does our constant racing around. To reduce this overwhelm, we need to go back to stillness and quiet.

Stillness lies at the heart of serenity, so to discover serenity in your life, make space for stillness and for peace and quiet each day, for a few minutes. There are countless ways of finding your path in life, but only one way of beginning to be still. It is universal, it can be known by anyone, it is the taste of silence, the creation of unity, the expression of harmony, when all the threads of silence that exist within all things of mind, body and the world reveal their structures and patterns to you.

FEAR OF FAILURE

The fear of failure leads directly to overwhelm. All too often fear of failure stops us in our tracks before we even begin. 'What if?' we tell ourselves, afraid to make mistakes, to fall or to admit defeat.

Yet there is one simple path that moves us towards success and away from fear and the overwhelm that goes with it – and that is to be prepared to fail and to continue on our path anyway. History is full of famous failures who refused to give up and found success in the end. Of course, it doesn't record the many millions who did give up and had to live with fear and regret.

The blueprint for success in the emotional and material world is to be prepared to fail at least twice as much as you did before. Failure is not, as many suppose, the enemy of success. Overwhelm is.

Failure is simply a test of your determination along the way to success. You can be downcast by failure – or you can gain knowledge from it. So make mistakes, with enthusiasm, for that is where you will ultimately find success. It is overwhelm and fear that cannot tolerate failure and mistakes. When you are not afraid to fail, overwhelm and fear lose their grip on you.

STRESS

Stress and overwhelm go hand in hand. We feel stressed when we get overwhelmed, and overwhelmed when we are under stress. Yet stress is not about the situation we find ourselves in, but our reaction to it.

When you find yourself feeling stressed, ask yourself: will this really matter in ten minutes, ten days, ten months or ten years from now? If the answer is no, as it is likely to be, then let it go. If it is yes, then do something about the situation.

Stress is simply the adaptation of our bodies and minds to change. If we find it difficult to cope with change, we become stressed. Yet we have within us the ability to control our reaction to change. We can react skilfully and positively, or unskilfully, causing damage to ourselves.

If you are suffering, your pain is not due to anything external, no matter how much you believe it is. It is caused by your attitude to it, and this you have the power to cancel at any moment. Do not expect problems or be anxious about what may never happen. If you focus on the possible when you experience difficult situations, you can positively change your outlook, reduce your stress, and concentrate on achieving things that otherwise may not have been possible. In the middle of difficulty lies opportunity.

Stress is the obsession of the everyday mind. Drop the idea that you alone are responsible for carrying the world on your shoulders. The world goes on without you. Do not regard yourself as so important.

Remember too that the time to relax is when you do not have time for it. The sign of a flourishing human being is one who can spend an entire day doing nothing without feeling guilty about it. It is a valid achievement equal to working hard. It is important to work for material success. It is also vital to take time off and to formulate your most important decision in the day by simply taking in the beauty of the sky, the smell of a good cup of coffee or the joy of other people's experiences.

Often, in my clinics, workshops, lectures and seminars in different parts of the world, people who are feeling overwhelmed sigh and say to me, 'Christopher, life is tough.'

I pause, then ask them, 'Compared to what?'

This often prompts tears or laughter. The truth is that life is life, and is the way it is. Sometimes life may seem beyond understanding and in those moments, do not try to understand – just accept. Life is telling you to pause and accept its cycles.

We live longer than our ancestors; yet we suffer from countless false fears and worries. Whereas our ancestors exhausted only their bodies, we burn the finer connections between the soul, mind, body, nerves and our place in the world. Is it worth doing this to ourselves?

One of the symptoms of feeling overwhelmed is the sad conviction that your work is very significant. Stress believes that life is an urgent situation and that the answer to this is to speed up and take on more. Yet the field of your everyday consciousness is small and can accept only one problem at a time. Slow down if you want to achieve more.

PEACE OF MIND IS A NATURAL STATE

For peace of mind, resign as general manager of the universe. You do not need to be in charge of everything all the time. Why not experience life free from worry? After all, if you treat every situation as a life-and-death matter, you will die many times, a series of small deaths that will cause you to have spiritual emergencies.

Do you feel that you are only doing something when you are worrying? There is an old Tibetan Bön saying: a grain store packed with worry will not pay a grain of debt.

Make the decision that any concern too small to be turned into an aspiration is too small to be made into a problem. A day of worry is far, far more exhausting than a day of work. Worry is rust upon your soul. Worry is a complete cycle of inefficient thought revolving around a pivot of fear.

Some patients I see are actually draining into their bodies the diseased thoughts of their minds, as they worry about the cares of tomorrow. Yet eventually all of our hurts and problems are survived or cured. We are more disturbed by a calamity that threatens us than by one that has befallen us, for grief has limits, whereas apprehension has none. Real difficulties can be healed; it is only the imaginary ones that are unconquerable.

Worry does not clear out tomorrow of its possible unhappiness; it abandons today, pilfering its strength. There are two days in the week on which I never worry: one is yesterday and the other is tomorrow. Follow this rule and you will learn that while fear tries to be in all things, serenity is already there.

Anxiety is a thin stream of fear trickling through the mind. If encouraged, it cuts a channel into which all other thoughts are drained. How do we encourage anxiety? Simply by focusing on it. And as we focus on it, we inevitably aren't focusing on solutions, joys and the things that make us feel happy.

There are people who are always anticipating trouble, and in this way they manage to enjoy many sorrows that never really happen to them. Only people obstruct happiness with worry, destroying what is with thoughts of what may be. Worry has far-reaching influence, invisible but very powerful. It steals your vitality and makes the physical pulse erratic; it diminishes your appetite, and turns the hair grey. If you believe that feeling bad or worrying long enough will change a past or future event, then you are on the first step to becoming ill. Worry affects the circulation, the heart, the glands and the whole nervous system. I have never known anyone who has really died from overwork, but many who have died from worry when overworking. We devour our tomorrows by fussing about our past. Nothing in the affairs of the manmade world is worthy of great anxiety. Look to your heart, be still, look into the serenity within; it is endlessly still, and it will reflect the truth of your life back to you.

Concern should drive us into action and not into a depression. You are not free if you cannot control your self. Fear nothing but what your approach to life may prevent; be confident of nothing but what opportunity cannot overcome. Worry is a thin stream of fear trickling through the mind. If encouraged, it cuts a channel into which all other thoughts are drained.

Early in my training I learnt the folly of worrying about anything. My master explained to me that there are only two things to worry about: either you are healthy or you are sick. If you are healthy, then there is nothing to worry about. If you are sick, there are only two things to worry about; either you will get well or you will die. If you get well, then there is nothing to worry about. If you die, there are only two things to worry about; you will go either to your idea of Heaven or to your idea of Hell. If you go to Heaven, then there is nothing to worry about. And if you to go Hell, you will be very busy indeed shaking hands with long-lost friends and worry will disappear! In addition, in Hell you will have the best opportunity to learn about Heaven and to go beyond it, whereas if you are in Heaven, you are in the status quo and that does not bring you spiritual development. So in the end there is nothing to worry about.

Since learning this, I have always worked as hard as I could, but when a thing went wrong and could not be righted, I dismissed it from my mind.

The Riverbank Story

In the Tibetan Bön tradition is this story about worrying. It is called 'The Riverbank Story'.

The winter was very harsh that year, and there was a great deal of rain and flooding. A merchant was on his way home when he saw in the valley below a number of people crossing what was a dry riverbed. Knowing this to be dangerous, he urged his servant to rush down to tell the people to hurry off the riverbed. But as the servant arrived, a great rumbling of floodwater, seething and turbulent, rushed along the riverbed, washing many away. Quickly, the servant and the merchant saved as many as they could. Bringing them on to the riverbank, the kind merchant gave them hot food and drink. But those who survived only worried about their situation and complained about the food, saying it had no taste, and the tea, which was not to their liking. The merchant was shocked that, having been saved from death, these people were worrying instead of giving thanks.

Shortly afterwards a Bön master walked past and consoled the merchant, saying to him, 'My friend, people get so in the habit of worry that if you save them from drowning and put them on a bank to dry, offering them hot tea and food, they will only wonder if they are catching cold. To save them from their folly is good, but to expect them to change because of that is not wise.'

The merchant was about to offer the master tea, but he was gone and the riverbed was dry.

'People worry because they think they must,' said the merchant's servant.

The merchant and his servant laughed and sat on the riverbank no longer worrying about the survivors, for all was well.

MEDIOCRITY

Feelings of overwhelm create mediocrity, when in fact we can, each one of us, be far more than we imagine. When we feel overwhelmed, we are paralysed, unable to meet challenges, stretch ourselves or achieve what we are capable of. We limit ourselves, allowing our fears to rule us.

Mediocrity requires aloofness to preserve its false dignity. There is nothing so useless as doing efficiently that which should not be done at all. And mediocrity excels in this. Give other people the freedom to lead small lives, but choose a big life for yourself. Allow other people to argue over small things, but not you. Do not judge other people when they cry over small hurts, but do not let yourself cry. Be tolerant of other people giving up their future into someone else's hands, but don't give up your own future.

Do not be afraid of tomorrow, for the divine in life is already there.

Fear can keep us up all night long, but faith makes a fine pillow on which to rest. Lay down your head upon that pillow of faith and kick every mediocre attitude out of the bed. Sleep a healing sleep bathed in faith. Faith keeps us in a wordless and profound conversation, intimate and immediate, with the natural world. Faith is not just a by-product of a belief in a god or religion, it is the state of the natural world.

You can find and develop faith and a knowing trust that

all will be well by going out into nature and immersing yourself in it. By gazing into the vastness of a blue sky and losing the repetitive chatter of your everyday mind, or by being part of the growing energy of a forest, or by merging your spirit with the surge of the sea. In paying respect to nature, you pay respect to yourself and know that you are part of nature too, and so faith is inspired. Anywhere there is nature there is the making of faith.

MEDITATION ON THE SEASONS

Spring comes with scents and blossoms bursting with life; summer brings us the playful breeze; autumn brings the golden mists; and winter the gift of powerful snow and the sudden darkness. We have much to learn from the seasons. The seasonal changes have a natural vitality in which worry has no place. Seasons follow a cycle, and if we allow ourselves to become one with this cycle, we will learn a great deal about our own nature.

Let us now focus upon the four seasons to understand the cycle of worry that may influence us through the year. Meditate on each description of the four seasons and let them create a response within you, letting the seasons come alive in your heart and mind. Spend ten minutes a day on one season, for a cycle of eight. Stop for seven days and then meditate for eight days on the next season, and so on. You can meditate on the inner season as and when you wish.

SPRING
Spring is bursting with life-giving force, eager to find release. Your mind, like the forces of nature, is being urged to awaken through your body to the new life that is streaming from the

earth. You can easily be overwhelmed in this season as every-thing is in transition and seems impetuous and short-lived. Spring is the impulse towards change. Here all your uncer-tainties are proved to be true or untrue.

Use this season to heal your fears of change and your fears of intimacy and friendship. Spring teaches you about the fleeting nature of beauty. The serenity that is offered through the qualities of spring is the serenity that knows all is essen-tially right with the world and nothing ever dies but merely changes its form.

SUMMER

Hot, brilliant, seemingly going on for ever, summer repre-sents the explosion and expansion into adoration of all things that are beautiful. Happy and healing, summer brings us the feeling of wellbeing but also offers us the illusion that life is unchanging. Summer offers us the serenity that everyone can find happiness, for it is his or her right and inner direction. Summer reassures that each of us has serenity within and that all our fears are merely steps to take us to a higher ground where our inner truth quietly waits for us to rediscover it. In this season we are taught the fears of impermanence and the heartbreak that comes when we truly experience the tran-sitory nature of all things.

AUTUMN

In autumn the world starts to shed what it no longer needs and silence is released from the flowers and flows out of the earth into the world of humankind. Autumn has come to teach us that all things in the world and within us have a beginning and an end. Yet this season can entrap us in attach-ment to the past while denying the future. Autumn is about the start of decay and how this belongs in the natural order of things. Autumn encourages you not to be trapped by your own fears but to understand them so that they may set you free from fear and small-mindedness. Autumn brings the message that nothing is isolated or separate, all things are connected. Autumn is the season that teaches self-reliance and offers the serenity of experiencing the connection of all life as a conscious but natural experience.

WINTER

Death, stillness, darkness, cold and retreat – these are the superficial expressions of winter. Winter allows the other three seasons to rest and regenerate, and it is in fact not the absence of life but the protector of life's impulse.

Winter's great gift to us is to teach us how to be still and enduring, regardless of what is going on around us. Winter shows us how to be strong and how to refuse to be overwhelmed by our fears, for fear can create winter within us. The serenity of winter brings the indestructible nature of wisdom, compassion and acceptance. Winter does not need to be anything but itself, and this is its lesson for us, for we should be the same.

THE INNER SEASON

Within each of us live the seeds of each season. Consider how each season makes you feel and during which season major events in your life have taken place. For instance, in which season were you born or have you married, had children or lived through other major life events? After considering each season and its connection to your life experiences, ask yourself what they have to teach you.

Through the year, on the first full moon of each season, focus on your life and the season's connection with you. The seasons will show you how your fears ebb and flow and how to find serenity, which quietly flows, connecting the seasons to make a perfect year of the unfolding soul.

Joe came to see me because he was troubled by repeated colds. He ran his own small delivery company and couldn't afford to take time off sick, yet the previous winter he'd suffered three colds in succession and had struggled with ill health for several weeks.

Joe wanted a fast-track to good health, but in looking at the causes of his colds, he was forced to confront the overwhelm he felt. Colds are often caused by overwhelm; they are the body's way of trying to force you to take time out. Like so many people, Joe was ignoring his body's message and driving himself on with increasing impatience.

When Joe talked about his life in more detail, he admitted that he felt constantly stressed, tired and worried. He didn't sleep well because he often lay awake anxiously planning his company's future and going over the finances, afraid that it might go under.

I asked Joe to take two weeks off work and during that time to hand over to his manager and have no contact with the business. He hadn't done this for ten years and was reluctant, but finally he agreed. I set him a daily timetable of walks in nature and told him to practise the Meditation on the Seasons, in particular the inner season.

Joe quickly came to understand, through his experience, how vital a connection with nature is to a sense of calm and wellbeing. After his two weeks off, he reorganised his life so that he regularly had time in the beautiful park near his home and beside the sea. He stopped believing that his company would collapse if he wasn't there – it had been fine in his absence – and began taking breaks and enjoying life away from work. He was delighted when the following winter he didn't have a single cold.

LISTENING

The act of listening holds the power to change your inner state. But how often do we truly listen? For most people the answer is never. All too often, instead of listening to what is being said to us, we are already listening in our heads to what we are going to say in reply. Most people will recognise this, having done it at some time or having experienced it while talking to another. When we do this, we block real communication.

When people talk, listen completely. If you listen completely, you actively dissolve obstructions and the feeling of being overwhelmed.

To listen closely and reply well is the highest perfection we are able to attain in the art of conversation. Often in life we want to hear something so badly that we allow our ears to betray our minds and our minds to deceive our hearts, in order to secure what turns out to be a false safety. We hear what we want to hear at the expense of the truth.

It is the province of knowledge and of opinion to speak, and it is the privilege of wisdom to listen. As you change your inner state, by truly listening, so your overwhelm will decrease.

The following exercise will help you to listen fully. You will be very surprised by what you hear.

The Listening Exercise

This simple exercise will clear away all the obstructions in your life caused by thoughtless words and unskilful thinking. Fear will lose its grip and serenity will be with you.

Sit quietly. Start to be aware of your surroundings. Listen to whatever is around you: noises, objects, people, the walls, space. Listen. Slowly breathe into the listening. Listen beneath the noise, the hum. Breathe in and rest.

Try this exercise whenever you have the opportunity, in order to increase and enhance your listening skills. Try it while listening to someone talking – on the radio, on television or in a real conversation. You will find that you sink beneath the words to the essence of what is being said. You will then see what people really mean and understand why they are saying what they are saying.

After having read through this chapter, go back to a part that calls you. Read it aloud and meditate on it. The section that attracts you is the one you most need to help heal fear and overwhelm and bring forth serenity.

8

LIFE, DEATH AND DYING

Throughout our lives each of us believes that we are learning how to live, but the reality is that we are actually learning how to die. We think, due to our fears, that life can be reduced to a set of rules, but in doing this, we fall into unconscious living. The more rules we create, the more habit-bound we become. And the more unconscious our life becomes, the stronger fear grows in our being. We lose innocence and spontaneity, we forget the light and vitality of life and we end up living in shadows.

Life is pure, knowing and changeable; it is captivating. Yet our fears would have us believe that life is completely the opposite, that fear is all there is, and of course the news on TV or in the newspaper seems only to confirm that this is true. However, life is greater than fear, for fear lasts only a short time, whereas life goes on beyond the imagining of fear, for ever.

Fear creates the belief that it is enduring, but the lessons of death and dying are that all things pass and that life itself is the great journey.

If you wish to know life intimately and directly, then eventually you must face up to what you fear about death. Death itself, which is but a chance to refresh and educate the soul, is not the issue, the fear of death is. In accepting, understanding and moving beyond your fear, your life changes and awakens to a constant state of joy, grounded in practical understanding of the daily world. People struggle so hard with the concrete, real and material that they forget the indefinable, the innocent, the knowing, the changeable, the enthralling. It is these that we must bring to death with us, for it is these that help us to die well. The way we live will inform the way we die. If we are able to live fully conscious, with an ever-deepening understanding of the interwoven nature of life and death, then we will die joyously and without fear.

Right now, pause, take a long breath in and out. Be as still as you can and read on.

Each section in this chapter is to be read as a meditation. It is a connection to the ongoing but unconscious awareness of the force of life within you and the experiences of death and dying that flow constantly within you and without, beneath every habit and facet of your everyday mind. In meditating on life and on death as you read the chapter, your awareness will grow and your fear diminish, so that you are able to move towards the joy of fearless living and dying.

LIFE

Life is in all places, sitting next to death. Life is everywhere. Life is death taking on another form. The Earth pulses with it. The plants, the creatures, visible and invisible, are filled with it. Life moves through them all like a wave, a sigh of constant energy. Life is also primeval, polluted and dirty. Even though we know this, we still want to be immersed in life. We have an instinctive urge to be in the heart of things. Through the desire to live, our life continues, which then brings us to the understanding of death and dying. Life seeks itself so that death and dying have their rightful place. In modern daily life death and dying are glossed over, relegated to something that happens to other people, sanitised, diminished in importance. In fact, as we shall see later in this chapter, death is at the heart of life.

People carry around so much pain in their hearts. The pain creates a veil that covers life. Life can be chaotic, hard to understand, without warning bringing blow after blow, just as it can bring wonder after wonder. Life is an unlimited communication in humility.

We live in an era of contradictions. We have more leisure but less time. We accumulate facts but have less sense, more knowledge but less understanding. In most societies we have increased our wealth but cheapened our principles. We gossip a great deal, love our fellow human beings infrequently and hate time and again. We've learnt to rush but not to wait. We have learnt to be hostage to our fears. We believe in the instant but not the long term.

Yet life continues to quietly encourage us to listen to it, as it really is, to listen, reclaim our humanity and be still. And while each of us constructs a life for ourselves, we receive the life we need.

Remember to cherish the life you have, take time to love, take care with the nature of your speech and take time to share the feelings in your heart. Your life is not measured by the number of days you live, but by the number of days in which you find wonder and reflection.

Know Your Purpose

The most important question you should ask is not how you will die but how you should live. For the manner of your life will determine the manner of your death. In determining how to live, you must find your life's purpose. In this way you will discover your inner greatness. Remember that each of us was not sent into this world to do anything into which we cannot put our heart. We live in an age of human history, particularly in our modern epoch, which is called 'dark', not because the human inner light fails to shine but because people refuse to see it. So many people are doing things in their lives without true heart or purpose. In this way they keep themselves in the dark. When you find your purpose, and follow it, your inner light will shine forth.

The most noble purpose of all, and the one that brings true happiness, is to serve others. Your deeds determine your person, as much as you determine your deeds. Forget yourself. Happiness comes when you are absorbed with something complete and satisfying that is outside the preoccupation with self. Everyone can be great, because everyone can serve.

The Four Beliefs of Fear

Bön practitioners say that when we live with fear as our guiding energy, there are four thoughts we are drawn to, which in turn become beliefs. They are known as the Four Beliefs of Fear. People choose these beliefs when they do not trust life and when they live with fear rather than with serenity. They hold these Four Beliefs of Fear to be true, they approach their life with these beliefs entrenched in their consciousness.

1. Life is an unbroken succession of false situations. Every opportunity is a false hope.

2. Life is tedious, just like a story, song or a joke that you have heard many times before.

3. Life is separated into the awful and the unhappy.

4. Life is jam-packed with wretchedness, isolation, and distress, and it's all over a great deal too soon.

Do you recognise any or all of these beliefs? Are they yours? Each of these four beliefs can reduce your experience and understanding of life and your role in life. The desire of life is to have you living in harmony, peace and consent with the natural world. When you are ruled by the beliefs of fear, this is not possible. The Invocation to Awaken Your Connection to Life, and the Meditation on the Source of Life that follow will help you to put your fearful beliefs to rest and focus instead on the serenity and joy life has to offer.

An Invocation to Awaken Your Connection to Life

Read this invocation out loud and then practise the meditation that follows. The invocation will act as a bridge between your everyday mind and your deeper consciousness. As you read it out aloud, it will profoundly awaken your connection to life, so that when you practise the meditation, your experience will be all the more immediate. Before you begin, concentrate on your breathing for a few moments.

> I live in celebration of all humankind
> In love with the visionary
> And the blind,
> The open heart and
> The closed one too
> For I am alive in the throng and hue of all
> The hum of the human race
> For in the centre

There lives a constant grace
For every heart
That beats its beat
I love humanity
I love . . .

In the anguish and the savagery
In the splendid and the morbid view
Human reason finds its way
In beauty and in light
Always there is the inner way
Covered often by the everyday
My joy is the joy of my fellow beings
The sparkle of all
Newborn dreams
I love the love that we all can know
The endless love that loves all.

Quiet, it will come
To doubters and believers it shows itself
For this inner love is all humankind,
Itself
Just is
Needs no now
No constant or tomorrow
Or endless vow
Receive it here
In your heart
For this is wisdom
Of the human way
Endless from all time
Beyond all space
It seeks the human

To make its place
Not mystic or the property of just a few
It opens the body to a newer world
It is love, and reason
Rhyme and beyond reason too
Delightful, severe, astonishing, new . . .
Human
Worldly
Yours
Mine
Truly
In all places . . .
Going
Coming
It arrives
Beyond
Before you leave
It's you, me, us and we
Enemy, friend
Them and us
Matter, dust
It comes, it's here
It heals all . . .

Living now
It lives through you
Sit be still and know this love
For it is life.

This is enough.

Meditation on the Source of Life

Sit in any position you wish and close your eyes. Listen to the noise around you, whatever it may be. Listen until you can listen 'inside' the noise, listen until all the noise becomes one hum, and then listen 'inside' the hum until all becomes silent. Listen to the silence until it erupts into a flame of clear light. Listen to the flame of clear light and allow it to enter into you. Become this flame of clear light. Allow the clear light to enter into the top of your head and see it flow slowly down your spine and then flow into your groin and from your groin up to your heart where it settles, infusing itself into your physical heart.

Do this meditation before sleep every night for as long as you wish.

DEATH

Death is more familiar than life, for everyone dies but not everyone makes a claim to life. Because people live as if they were dead to life, they become afraid and serenity is hard to experience. Do not fear death but rather the aloof and fearful life.

Death is certain for all creatures born in this world, so what is the point of grief and worry? When faced with death, give thanks for the continuation of the cycles of birth and death and for the wisdom, love and serenity that comes from that.

The person not engaged in the daily experience of being alive to the offering of life each day is busy dying of the suffocation of habit and fear. Be open to people. Embrace each and every one. Because our life is over all too soon.

No one should leave this life with unfinished business. Unfinished business of the mind, the heart, life and work attracts fear in the same way as whistling to a dog will attract it. Unfinished business causes you to be unfinished; your soul is left unrealised and partially alive.

So take time to complete what you have begun and to be open, honest and clear with every person that you can. When you do this, fear will disappear and serenity will become the language of respect and truth between all people.

The Soldier's Story

I spent twelve years of my life resolutely learning how to kill, carrying out deadly missions, fighting hand to hand to conquer the enemy, to send them to their deaths or running in fear. I was not going to roll over and surrender. My anger was part of the crusade to fight death . . . which I believed in with absolute certainty.

Then suddenly one day all the death I had caused came up and slapped me across the face. I saw how wrong I was and how the death I had caused was theft. Yes, killing is theft. I had misunderstood the nature of death, believing it was justifiable.

In all the cities, countries, dangerous and mad places in which I had fought and killed, I thought I was trying to bring order and a better way of life, but I became horrified by what I had done. It was as though I had awoken from a dream.

I cannot give back the lives I took, but I know now that it is life that's important. Now I strive every day to be a compassionate, big-hearted, caring person. Anytime I even think about getting angry with anybody, I see death and I remember: life is everything.

This soldier's experience is, unfortunately, very common now in all areas of conflict in the world, as it has been throughout history. The catalyst that changed him so deeply was that he had a face-to-face encounter with death, but it was not the version of death that he had in his mind and belief system. The death he met showed him the effects of all those lost lives upon the planet as a whole. This terrified the soldier, it humbled him, and he gave up the spirit of killing.

Those trained to take life so often live to regret it, as they come to understand that life is sacred and death no solution at all. For this soldier the unfinished business of his life – regret over the deaths he had caused – could only be completed by living the rest of his life in as honest and compassionate a way as he possibly could.

Fear of Death

So many people fear the solitude of death. This, ironically, is a common bond that we all have in life. Yet there is nothing to fear in death, for when death has come, we are no longer. Death is impersonal, it is only our experiences and fears around it that give it personal meaning.

The cure for fear of death is to take joy in the freedom that comes from the lessons that life can teach us, fleeting as it may be. I once said to a famous patient who was going to die and needed a sense of connection to the deeper reality in his life, 'George, three days after passing away, your hair, bones and fingernails will keep on growing, but all your phone calls will stop.' He got the point and laughed and his death, soon afterwards, was serene.

Love of this world never dies a physical death. It dies because we do not know how to replenish its source. It dies from a lack of personal vision, self-important attitudes and inner dishonesty. There is no goal better than this in this material world: to know on your deathbed that you lived your life in accordance with the goodness that is within you and that you did what made you happy, accepting full responsibility for your actions.

We often think that death is final. Yet in so many ways it is not. Death ends the physical existence you have had, but the energy of the relationships you have made lives on. To understand death, it important to realise that we must love one another or depart this life unhappy. If we die unhappy, our death will not be fulfilled but tired and empty. And when this happens, it is a great sadness, for we are unable to experience the full joy that death may bring. This is the only aspect of death that we should ever fear.

To die is simply to let your body dissolve back into its own components, the earth, sky, wind, sun, moon and all of nature. The day of death, which we fear as our last, is but the remembering of eternity. Death does not and cannot extinguish our inner light, for death is merely the equivalent of turning off the light in the room because morning has crept in through the windows.

If you allow your mind to be made small by fear, it will shrivel, but if your inner heart is strong and direct, then your most important beliefs will transform your death. In the experience of death, imagination is stronger than information, your own personal story more potent than the past. Trust the redemptive power of your imagination and understand your own myth that you have made in order to live each day. Dreams are more powerful than facts in this experience, hope triumphs over any negative experience of life, and love is stronger than a fearful death. Knowing this within brings serenity.

Taking Time to Reflect

In all our thoughts and activities it is worth reflecting on the following fact: what we have made for ourselves dies with us and is forgotten, while what each of us does for others finds its way into everyone's hearts and so becomes perpetual.

Life is for ever, and death is only an opportunity to pause and reflect, reform yourself and continue on, refreshed. When, at the point of death, you look back at your life, what would you like to see? What would make you most proud, most happy and most satisfied? Would it be a lifetime of long hours in the office? A smart house and an expensive car? Or would it be the connections you have made with others, the bonds with those you love, and what you have been able to give to others?

Do you believe that when you die, what has happened during your life won't matter, because death is like a final sleep? If so, then you are simply turning away from the truth. Death is not the end of everything, it is in fact the prime awakening of our souls.

Death is a separation of your energy and your body, a metamorphosis of our human nature, merging with eternity. Death is the most beautiful adventure in life. Life is eternal and love is immortal, and it is in death that we have the chance to embrace these. Death is an accelerated path to self-knowledge, a means of comprehension and understanding limited only by the nature of our inner vision.

Death is a release from pain. Whatever hardship, evil or pain may have happened to you in life will not stay with you; death lets it go, its lessons learnt.

An Invocation of Understanding: The Story of Life and Death

Every morning, as you wake, read this traditional Tibetan story aloud:

A man woke from his sleep one night when the world was still and he called out, 'Life, I want to hear Death speak and release its mysteries to me.'

The wind fluttered through the moonlit leaves. From out of the hush, Life raised her voice and sang, 'You hear him now.'

All was silent, the world paused. Then a low, quiet voice whispered in the heart of the man, 'Birth and death are the two most elegant expressions of the courage that is needed to live a full life. A life full of desire. Desire is part of life, indifference is part of death. Even at our conception, death waits quietly in the shadows, not bringing fear but joy. For death is a lover of life. Every day death looks towards us and we look at death but only see fear, while death looks at us, sees our humanity, our frailty but offers us the chance to know our serenity. Our fear of death is momentary.

'Just as we talk fondly of the summers that have faded and gone, their warmth now part of our souls, so it is with our good actions. They stay in the memory of our life and death. The path to a skilful death is to live a good and generous life.'

The man was enraptured by the words of Death, and as he sighed, taking in the importance of these words, Death continued, 'Do not become caught up in what you own or who you love at the time of death. The most important thing is to care about the utmost development of your soul. All other things at this time become difficulties, beset with fear and frustration. The difficulty is not in avoiding death, but in avoiding unskilfulness in death. Death is a pause so that your soul might catch its breath for the great journey forward.'

At that the man knew the greatest peace he had ever known, and death came to him. All was serene.

Ancient Tibetans believed that upon death they would be asked two questions and their answers would decide whether they could continue their voyage to the spirit world. The first question was 'Did you bring joy?' The second was 'Did you find joy?' There were no wrong answers. Only learning.

Meditation on Death

Sit quietly and follow your breathing, allowing your body to be comfortable. As you do this, see yourself dead, with all those people that you honestly love around you. See your body decaying and turning to dust, but within the dust there shines a pulsing, clear light. See those assembled loved ones also die and turn to dust, and there too shines the same clear light. Suddenly all the clear lights merge into one clear light. All that exists is serenity and a powerful gentleness.

Practise this meditation when you first wake up, for ten minutes. When you have finished, give thanks for every day of your life.

DYING

Death is a liberation. It is dying that's difficult. For dying is a process, as life is, and this process is not always easy or clear.

In this section of the chapter let us explore the attitudes and fearful patterns of life that stop us from experiencing the beauty of dying and what it has to teach us, each day and at the end of our lives. Dying is an expression of life, but a life that you have forgotten in order to experience the material world. The following five steps will help you to understand the nature of dying. Reading them aloud is a form of meditation, so sit peacefully and read each one aloud, quietly but clearly. They may make no sense to your rational mind, but be patient and you will find that the sense of each will become clear.

The Five Steps to Understanding the Nature of Dying

STEP ONE

A human being is part of a whole, the whole is called the 'universe'. Each human is a dimension limited in time and space. We experience ourselves and our thoughts and feelings as something separate. But this is a mirage, a shadow play that we create through fear, in order to contain our consciousness. This delusion is captivity for us, restricting us to our personal desires and to affection for those close to us. Our undertaking must be to free ourselves from this captivity by widening our circles of compassion to embrace all living creatures and the whole of nature in its beauty. A person starts to live fully when he or she can live outside this personal captivity. This first step is the first part of understanding how the experience of death and dying leads us to self-knowledge.

STEP TWO

The inherent wisdom in life goes beyond a personal deity and steers clear of doctrines and theology. It covers both the natural and the spiritual, and is based on the experience that comes from the understanding of all things as a meaningful unity. This then is the next crucial step: what do you believe in?, what primal fear attaches itself to your beliefs?

STEP THREE

It is the responsibility of each of us to break free from our fear and to find inner freedom. To do this, we need imagination, for while knowledge is limited, imagination encircles the world. We can use our imagination to recognise the greater whole, of which each one of us is a part. Thus in dying, we free our imagination from fear and allow it an unhindered experience of our greater states of awareness that dying and death offers each of us.

STEP FOUR

Life is like crossing a river over a number of stepping stones. To keep your balance, you must keep moving. Death is not falling off, it is a change in how you use energy. Dying is not a loss of control, merely a change of pace.

STEP FIVE

The distinction between past, present and future is only a stubbornly persistent illusion. And dying is also an illusion, just as physics states time to be. Only a life lived for others brings true understanding to the process of dying.

The Three Common Confusions

There are three common origins of confusion in people's lives that cause the fear of life, death and dying. They are:

1. Worry.
2. Anger.
3. Despair.

Pause for a moment to consider how each or one of these three influences your life. It is likely that one of these is the main theme of your life. Are you a worrier? Are you an angry person? Or do you despair? Whichever may be true of you, know that all three arise through fear. These are such subtle and pervasive fears that they alter and rearrange the life you have and will have. But when there is a fear of dying, one of these three has created the fear.

WORRY

When worry is the main influence in your life, it is because you feel trapped, bound by fears you cannot understand. You will always find something to worry about, for you strive for perfection but worry that you will never achieve it. Of course you are right, worry never achieves perfection, only worry. The fear that causes worry comes from a desperate need to make the world safe around you. To heal this fear, you need to focus on times in your life when while facing great difficulties, you have experienced unexpected good fortune that has kept you safe and sound.

ANGER

Anger becomes angry because of itself. The angrier you become, the angrier you will be and the more your fear will control your emotional make-up. Anger seeks meaning in everything; it wants to know the how and why of every subject. It is not content just to be. It encourages change, movement and enquiry in order not to look at itself and find its own faults. If you feel that anger is your motivating force in life, then to conquer this fear, you need to experience the nature of forgiveness. Forgiving yourself for anger and knowing that all your experiences of life can be enriched by love will be your path to healing.

DESPAIR

Despair is the emotion that brings us closest to a state of feeling dead. When we are in despair, we are numbed and dulled. Despair cannot see beyond its own suffering, because it does not know anything other than itself. It is unskilful self-absorption, a form of suffering that clings to any type of life force or vitality in order to know that it suffers. If you view the world from the vision of despair, then to transform this fear, you need to learn the skill and wisdom of living one day at a time and seeing the good in people. In doing this, you begin to regain a sense of yourself.

In the Tibetan Bön teachings on dying each of the Three Common Confusions can make the dying process a terrifying, unhappy experience that seriously unbalances the mental forces that survive the death of the body. Each one of these can dominate you, directing you immediately back into birth again, robbing you of the opportunity of facing the divine directly and healing your powerful fears.

Meditation on Dying

Use the following meditation on dying to address your worry, despair or anger and the fear of death it has engendered.

Close your eyes. In your mind, see a fresh shiny leaf attached to a tree. See the leaf fall from the tree, falling slowly to the ground. As it falls, it starts to change, it loses its vitality, it withers, and the body of the leaf dries and becomes brittle. It touches the ground, merging with all the other leaves. You find yourself looking up at the tree and, to your wonder, there is the spirit of the leaf, a shape not unlike its former body, still attached to the tree. It is luminous, living and bright. Through the leaf you see that dying is the loss of the body but the realisation of its content, its innermost nature. At this point give thanks for dying and open your eyes.

Life, death and dying are inextricably connected. Serenity is their common ground; fear is what makes us hold back from them. Take your time in re-reading this chapter, following it step by step, and your own inner wisdom and understanding on this subject will awaken and begin to teach you directly. There is no death, no dying, only life and living.

Meditation to Bring Comfort to the Dying

This meditation can be read aloud to someone who is close to death. You can also simply read it to yourself on behalf of someone who is dying, if you are not with them. If you are doing this, simply direct the energy of the meditation to the dying person.

It can also be of help to those who have lost loved ones.

Feel your body, it is like a veil from behind which there shines a light. Feel your breath, it is like a veil from behind which there shines a light. Breathe in and out slowly. Let the light of your body and the light behind your breath become as one clear light. As the two lights merge, peace and mental clarity appear and encompass your body and mind. Stillness and wellbeing are everywhere, within you and all around you. Rest quietly. The clear light comes to you. Your fear is washed away, you can move forward, on to new choices, experiences and blessings.

All her life Marina was afraid of death and of the end of 'her'. When she was dying, at the age of sixty, her fear was still with her. I gave her the Meditation to Bring Comfort to the Dying, and as she read it to herself over and over, her fears evaporated. In the last few days of her life she became a different person. Her family noticed that she was happier, lighter, more playful and optimistic. Marina had had a serious life, working as a judge. Yet in her last days joy, lightness and self-knowledge were her gifts to her family and friends.

Time to Let Go

Death is not our final experience, nor is it the end. It is merely a process by which you come back to knowing who you really are and can be. The hardest part of the experience of dying is letting go of all the fear that it brings. When people are afraid of death, it is not death they are afraid of but the opportunities for change and self-knowledge that accompany dying. If you are dying now, or afraid of death, remember that death is a natural part of life. Have courage, embrace what comes to you and your fear will melt away.

One of the greatest opportunities death offers is the chance to make peace with our past. All people can overcome their past when they die. If you have done things in your life that you are ashamed of – and which of us has not? – then you have the opportunity to put things right. You need first to forgive yourself for your shame. If you can contact the people that you feel you have wronged and ask for forgiveness, then do so. If you cannot, then ask the person out loud to forgive you; you will sense their forgiveness coming back to you. The natural movement of consciousness is towards serenity, balance and order, and forgiveness is part of that. Feel the love that lives in all things. Try to become as the love is. Finally, know that the things you are ashamed of were lessons you needed to learn. Now you have learnt them, let them go and focus upon the goodness in your heart.

Cody worked in the corporate world, a real high-flying, 'take no prisoners' kind of guy. When he was diagnosed with pancreatic cancer and learnt that he did not have long to live, all the dark things he had done in his life came rushing back to him. Cody was filled with shame and horror at some of his misdeeds, knowing that he had lied, conned and manipulated others to get what he wanted. His unhappiness at what he had done was standing in the way of a peaceful death.

After we had talked, Cody set about asking for forgiveness from those he had wronged. In one or two cases he was able to contact the person directly. In most cases he could not, but he placed the person in his mind and asked for their forgiveness. As he did this, Cody was able to forgive himself and to see the vital lessons he had learnt and would take with him.

Cody died with peace and self-respect, having discovered the well of goodness he held inside. He had learnt that life could be good, whole, safe and innocent. His fear had passed away and he died happy and serene.

9

FAILURE AND SUCCESS

The notions of failure and success are hugely important in today's society. We judge ourselves and others according to our ideas of what constitutes failure or success. When we decide that someone is a success, we applaud them and envy them. When we condemn another person as a failure, we avoid them and pity them. Yet our notions of failure and success are extremely limited and are inextricably linked with poverty and prosperity.

A man or woman who makes a great deal of money, owns many possessions and can wield power over others is considered a success, regardless of whether or not this person is happy, fulfilled, self-aware or kind to others. A person who is contented, at peace with themselves, generous and spiritually aware may still be considered a failure if he or she is poor and has few possessions.

How have we created such distorted notions? The answer is through fear. It is fear that drives us to believe that however much we have, it is still not enough. Fear propels us towards money and the belief that money buys happiness and that if we acquire more and more we will eventually feel satisfied. Myths such as this have arisen over the last few hundred years and now dominate most societies in the world. We only have to look around us to see that many well-off people are unhappy. Yet we still long to be as well off as they are, believing that for us it would be different, we would be contented with our lot.

When we narrow our vision in this way, we ignore so much that is good and valuable. We forget the joy that lies in our relationships with others, in meaningful endeavour, in being generous and in developing a strong inner life.

Unfortunately, we are encouraged, particularly in Western societies, to view success and failure in these limited ways. All around us the myths of success and failure are reinforced, through newspapers, television, popular songs and advertisements. People who earn a great deal of money are labelled as a 'success' automatically, no matter how grey and anxious their visages. Others, who do not fit in with society's rules by being ambitious or acquisitive, are labelled 'odd', 'failures', 'misfits' and 'dropouts'. Ultimately, the fear of success and failure has acquired an unparalleled power to arouse misery, anguish and pain.

In this chapter I will challenge many of the myths we have about success and failure and I will examine the value of failure and the true meaning of success. I will also look at the links between failure and success, and prosperity and poverty, and the role of money in our lives. By understanding the role fear may play in your own view of success and failure, you will be in a position to reassess the choices you have made and to make fresh choices about the way you wish your life to move forward.

THE LEGACY OF FEAR

The world has become driven by an upswell of fear, which is even stronger now than in the past. This is because of the enormous growth in wealth since the Second World War, and the association that has been created between wealth, morality and emotional wellbeing. The spiritual and psychological pressures placed upon society at large and on individuals by this process has created more and more fear, as people feel less connected to who they really are. The rapid state of growth has literally created a rapid growth of fear. And the more fear grows, the more we connect money and wealth with inner value and self-worth, leading to a crippling and utterly false view of success and failure.

It is only in the last 350 years that, in the West and increasingly worldwide, success and failure have become directly linked to money in this way. Before this, notions of success and failure were far broader, and encompassed achievements other than those which made money. But as the connection with money has become stronger, so there has been an increasing growth of fear in the world with regard to money. And as this has continued, the black-and-white view of success and failure has gained an unskilful moral influence.

Because of the endemic attitude that money is success, most people set out to make money. They take jobs they might not enjoy, work long hours and put up with being treated badly in the workplace, all in order to make as much money as possible. As a result many people on the ladder to 'success' become addicted to the fearful side of success and failure – terrified of failing and clinging precariously to what 'success' they have. And in the end their fear can literally make them sick. The stress of living in a constantly fearful state leads to illness, breakdown and unhappiness.

The myths that have been created include those that say anyone can – and should – be successful and rich, no one has to be poor, nothing is ordained in life, and everyone had a chance of being a winner.

The result is that many people, as they struggle to prove their value to the world, become resentful of the successful, scornful of the 'failures' and ashamed of themselves.

INNER WORTH

The path to finding true success and to banishing the fear of failure is to know your own inner worth.

False success can swindle your soul. Inner worth liberates it. Inner worth knows your fears and uses them daily, transforming them into productive and useful energy and knowledge.

Success of any kind is short-lived; there is no such thing as enduring or permanent success. If, instead of valuing the success we have, we simply chase after more success, it will only bring with it more fear and certain failure. Failure presents itself to stop you in your tracks so that you may know yourself, this is its great value. It is through your failures that you can discover your inner worth. As your sense of inner worth becomes stronger, you will find that you deal with failure better, never allowing it to defeat you, and that you attract success and good fortune.

Meditation for Discovering and Strengthening Inner Worth

Inner worth is what you are born with. It is all your essential goodness, talents, compassion and self-discipline, plus the ability to love everyone spiritually because you recognise your inner worth in others and theirs in you.

This meditation is very simple and it will help you to rediscover the inner worth you already have.

Sit still and close your eyes. Tune in to the emotions and energy of other people. Feel everything they feel. Do not judge or become involved in what you sense, feel or experience. Be observant, and as you do this, feel the impartial compassion within you rise up and allow it to surge through you, to others.

Do this for at least twenty minutes a day, as often as you wish. The ideal time to do it is just after waking, before eating or drinking.

When you activate your inner worth, people will relate to you more easily and you will have a greater sense of completeness. You are becoming more human, discovering freedom and serenity. Obstacles will not seem so daunting, and you will become happier with yourself. You may also find that you wish to change your lifestyle in order to accommodate this new-found inner worth. Treat it as a sacred treasure. Do not squander it or let anyone else destroy it. Those people who do not respect or acknowledge their inner worth may try to belittle yours – do not allow them to.

THE BLESSINGS OF SUCCESS AND FAILURE

Despite the myths perpetuated by society, which we can challenge once we understand that they are only myths, the successes and failures in our own lives have much to teach us.

Success and failure can reveal serenity to you at the point when you come to realise your place in your own life. This happens in the quiet moments when success comes to you and you feel fulfilled or when failure teaches you acceptance.

We have endless opportunities for advancement and failure, and they are to be found in that opening of radiance when we look within and know ourselves to be the creators and destroyers of the impulse of our own lives.

TRUE SUCCESS

Success is the benefit you will receive when you are able to just be yourself, without adornment or artifice, in your chosen area of activity. To perform any activity, whether paid or unpaid, wholeheartedly, with attention and pleasure, will result in success. Lasting success comes from the experience of expressing all you are and can be.

If your success is not based on your own skills and integrity, if it looks superficially good to the world but does not feel genuine and good to your inner self, it is not success at all but rather a false situation made by fear.

The secret of success is to experience unconditional acceptance of life and what it brings, every single day. If you can accept everything that comes to you, both good and bad, easy and difficult, with the same calm and positive attitude, then you have found success. If you have an open heart, you will know that however difficult your circumstances they still offer you opportunities for growth, learning and success.

Opportunity often comes in disguise to test your resolve and ability to adapt.

Real success lies in finding the lifework that you feel is true to who you are and then being willing to overcome obstacles and persevere with whatever challenges you are given.

Success in any human activity requires preparation and instruction, self-control and effort. If you have these, the opportunities for healing your fears of success and the gloom of fear are instant.

Beware, though, of the search for perfection. To want to do something as well as you possibly can is admirable, but to insist on striving for perfection is ultimately destructive.

The search for perfection becomes a fearful and consuming process, and perfection and success when mixed together bring suffering, for the possibility of material perfection is an illusion perpetuated by fear.

In your life's endeavours never strive for success. True success is that which comes as a by-product when you strive for awareness, compassion and love. In all your activities allow your goodness to direct your intention. The superficial world loves success as long as it fits into the narrow classification of what success should be. But true success is beyond labelling because it is as individual as every man, woman and child on this small planet.

Success for each of us can be many things, but the success we can all hope to attain is the ability to move from failure to failure with no loss of self-love. If you can do this, the path to success becomes a spiritual path in its own right, one that every human being must go through in his or her life, on the journey to self-knowledge.

Never accept the illusion that success is the achievement of all your dreams. It is not. Rather it lies in knowing how to dream, while discovering the serenity that enables you to deal with everything life throws at you, without losing the beauty of who you are.

THE VALUE OF FAILURE

Many people give up just before they achieve what they set out to do. They lose faith and cannot believe that they will really manage it. The result is that many people who feel they are failures are those who did not realise how close they were to success when they gave up. Giving up just before attainment comes within your reach is a hard loss to carry.

Many people are bowed down by the 'if onlys' of life and feel guilty, regretful, resentful or bitter.

Yet there is no need to be depressed by failure, for it is actually a life-affirming experience. In fact, failure is what leads us on the road to success, because each detection of what is unskilful or false in our search for success leads us to seek more carefully for what is skilful and real.

Every time we falter, make a mistake or fall, we learn something new. Each dead end indicates a new direction, each mistake shows us what to avoid in the future. This occurrence that we call 'failure' is not the falling down but the staying down. If you believe that defeat is your destiny, then you allow yourself to fail. If you treat each failure as a stepping stone on the path to success, then success is yours. Failure tricks us into believing that we have been forced to climb down the ladder of success to the lowest rung. All too often we believe that our failure reflects our inner worth. The shadow of failure is the feeling of inferiority it can bring. While success is a hopeful energy, it can diminish in the face of failure, if we allow it to. Failure is no more than an expression of grief, while success is an abundant shaft of light that creates good things. When you fail, it is the failure of the unknowing part of you, the part that chooses ignorance over knowledge. When you succeed, it is because you refuse to allow failure to be all that you are and move forward with optimism and courage.

Why do we fail?
Is it because we are unlucky?
Is it because we have not worked hard enough?
Is it because we have not invoked holiness within ourselves?
Is it because we are not good enough, clever enough or talented enough?
Is it because it is our destiny?

We give ourselves all these reasons, and many more, as explanations of our failures. Yet none are true.

The inner wisdom of our most sacred self bequeaths us the wisdom of loss and failure for the strengthening of our consciousness.

Why do we succeed?

Is it because we are fortunate?

Is it because we have worked very hard?

Is it because the divine forces of nature are kind to us or because we have a special connection to whatever god we believe in?

Is it because we are talented, clever or good?

Is it because it is our destiny?

No, it is not because of these things that we achieve success.

We succeed because our inner wisdom attracts success to us – the success to educate and support us and to make us stronger.

Failure strengthens our consciousness if we learn from it and heal the fear that makes us prone to failure. Success educates and supports us and makes us stronger only if we are thankful and respectful for it and share it with others. Success can turn to failure if we do not share the positive energy behind it, which is our inner wisdom.

WITNESSING CONSCIOUSNESS

When we achieve serenity, we accept both failure and success as part of life. Our failures do not bow us down, and our successes do not fool us. We know that both will come and go many times, weaving through the pattern of our lives. Serenity lifts us above both failure and success, so that we meet them both with love. When our inner life is rich and fulfilled, we are less dependent on outer successes and failures. They no longer define us, control us or dictate our path. One of the most powerful ways to develop your inner serenity is to practise what the ancient Tibetan Bön teachers called 'witnessing consciousness'. The Bön practitioners knew that love and hate, as well as success and failure, were simply two sides of the same coin. Witnessing consciousness is a way of rising above the thunderstorm of emotions, the extremes that love and hate, or failure and success can take us to – extremes of despair, longing, rejection, pain and misery.

Societies, nations and races have a shared consciousness or unconsciousness, but it is the individual alone who can enter into the realm of witnessing consciousness. Through witnessing consciousness, the spiritual energy of the individual grows, and this spiritual growth becomes a shining example.

Practising Witnessing Consciousness

Witnessing consciousness is learning how to observe the way your thoughts react to everything that you experience. It is not the observation of the deepest inner self but of the everyday mind and the way its reactions create fear.

It can be done at any time, for it is simply trying to consciously observe the way you react to the world around you and to people and events. It is the study of your own reactions. All you do is examine how reactive you are. Look at what sparks your emotions, opinions and habits.

If you wish to develop the practice of witnessing consciousness, do it every day, as constantly as you can, for twelve days. After that, reflect on your observations for a three-day period, and then do it again for a twelve-day period. Repeat this cycle at least six times a year. It will bring you valuable awareness about the way your consciousness works in the everyday world.

Danny was so reactive and even aggressive that he started to drive his friends and loved ones away. He would leap to defend himself or attack the other person over what seemed to others to be quite inoffensive observations or remarks. The result was that people around him backed off or became ultra-cautious when they were with him.

Danny knew that his responses had developed in child-hood. He was constantly criticised by his parents, and the result was that he had become critical and defensive himself. But knowing why he behaved in the way he did hadn't helped him to stop.

When I met Danny, he was feeling desperate. His girl-friend has just told him that unless he changed she would leave him. I taught Danny how to practise witnessing consciousness and explained that in objectively observing his behaviour and reactions, he would learn a great deal and begin to see that he had choices.

Danny began with enthusiasm and soon noticed patterns of reactive behaviour that stopped other people from commu-nicating with him. Once he had done this, he was able to interrupt his reactions and choose to behave differently.

All this took him a while – changing behaviour is not easy. But he was determined and was encouraged when his new behaviour drew warm responses from others. His girl-friend was delighted with the softer, more open man he became, and their relationship became more satisfying for both of them.

ATTITUDE

Your attitude to life and to success and failure is vitally important.

A positive and encouraging mental attitude will create more miracles than any wonder drug. By changing the inner attitude of your mind, you can change the outer aspects of your life far more effectively than by struggling only to make outer changes.

The greatest discovery of our times is that a human being can alter his life by altering his mental attitude. Yet this is not a new discovery. Wise people, including the Bön practitioners, have always known it. They understood, long before today's spate of self-help books were written, that a positive mental attitude was more crucial than any other attribute on the path to happiness. We all encounter difficulties and troubles, confusions and obstacles. When we meet them stubbornly and defiantly, attempting to break through them with the force of our will, we are ineffectual. However, when we learn to meet them gently and with compassion, without hurrying or forcing, we learn that in time they will bend.

A strong and optimistic mental attitude is part of the cycle of cause and effect. What you give out will define what comes back to you. So be gracious to everyone, good company to many, known to a few, companion to one, enemy to none. A strong mental attitude acknowledges that nothing in life is certain, save that we were born and will die. Uncertainty and impermanence are part of the fabric of life. Change is all around us, in the weather, in the seasons and in our lives. When we learn not to fear change but to recognise that it is fundamental to life, then we become strong, self-aware and able to cope with whatever change brings.

A positive mental attitude will engender in us the desire to be kind to others. And kindness has extraordinary power, in our individual lives and in the world around us. Kindness can conquer the pain of failure and the blindness made by fearful success. Share goodness with others, be kind to yourself and to those around you, and the darkness in the world, caused by belief in fear, will turn to the light of serenity.

POVERTY AND PROSPERITY

Poverty and prosperity are inextricably linked with success and failure in the eyes of modern society. The beliefs that if you are prosperous, you are a success, and if you have poverty, you are a failure are powerful. So powerful that most of us are conditioned to the point that we feel that what we have is who we are and that we will be judged by others on this basis alone.

This is a sad and limiting belief and one that you need to let go of. There is nothing wrong with success or prosperity, as long as you can stand back from it and see that it is is simply passing through your life and nothing to do with the essential you.

When prosperity comes into your life, give thanks for it but do not use all of it. Instead, save some and give some away. If you save some of what comes to you, then you will always feel prosperous, knowing that you have surplus put by. And if you give some of what you have to others in need, then you create the energy of renewal.

Earth provides sufficient to satisfy every person's need but not everyone's greed. Therefore it is vital that we do not plunder the Earth's resources simply for the sake of having more. Each one of us can contribute to caring for the Earth, by using what we have with care, never wasting food, water and other precious resources.

The belief that we are entitled to more than enough is in fact creating a kind of poverty – the poverty of those who cannot be content with what they have. This is the poverty of the modern era. Many people ignore what they already have in the pursuit of more. With this kind of mentality nothing is ever good enough, expensive enough or big enough. Homes, cars and clothes become status symbols we compete over rather than the necessities of life we appreciate and give thanks for.

To have less when you can get more is the great challenge of modern times. In past eras this was possible only for a very few. But now many people have to face this dilemma.

The gap between what we have and what we think we ought to have is an ethical problem, not an economic one, a problem created by fear. Only fear drives us to take for granted all that we have and crave more.

The rampant fear of poverty among educated social groups is the worst spiritual disease from which our current mode of civilisation suffers. With this disease a rich person is often just a poor person with wealth.

To be content with what you have, the simplest thing to do is say, 'Thank you,' out loud, every day, for all that you have. The more you say it, the more content you will be.

ACHIEVEMENT

If you have the ability and skill to get something done and the staying power to stick with your task, then you are on the path to achievement. The important thing in life is to decide what is worth achieving and what is not. For this, you must know what really matters to you, what your hopes and dreams are and what your challenges are.

Many of life's greatest achievements are not material ones. For some, the height of achievement is to climb a mountain; for others, it is to overcome some kind of adversity or illness. Others achieve spiritual development, educational goals or a harmonious relationship. All of these and many more are life's wondrous achievements.

Always value your own achievements and applaud those of others, sharing in their sense of accomplishment and pride. Remember that in the search for genuine achievement, you will experience competition. But competition should be a by-product of productive work, not its goal. A creative person is encouraged by the desire to achieve, not by the desire to beat others. If you are pushed to beat others, then it is fear that you are gathering to you, and it will cause you to lose the connection to your inner serenity.

In our greatest achievements we push back the boundaries of what we believe we can do and find in ourselves strength of character, willpower and a courage we didn't know we possessed.

All true achievement is carried out with love. Achievement without love is empty and attracts fear. Love is the spark that ignites true achievement, and achievement is the fire that grows from love's spark.

In Bön belief there are seven steps we need to take to any true achievement. If you follow these steps, they will take you to your goal.

The Seven Steps to Achievement

1. Learn how to make decisions that are free of fear, so that your progress shall be clear.

2. Choose pursuits – whether at work or play – that you love and give them the best there is in you.

3. Seize your opportunities based upon a clear and serene mind.

4. Learn to live in perfect comfort with your higher levels of power.

5. Know that there are mental and spiritual energies dormant in you that will only wake when there is need.

6. Be willing to go beyond your limits.

7. Be prepared to fail greatly so that you can achieve greatly.

Consider each of these seven steps carefully. Which ones do you need to focus on the most?

The more serene and free from fear you are, the easier you will find it to follow these steps and to achieve your goals.

Thought Exercise

Just before going to sleep, focus upon your heartbeat and clear your mind. Now direct your imagination to achievement and consider the possibilities of tomorrow. Imagine all ideas of hardship, worry or fear being decisively extinguished, to be replaced by courage, boldness and good humour. Now focus on whichever of the Seven Steps to Achievement seems most unattainable to you. Imagine yourself taking this step and making it part of who you are.

THE ROLE OF MONEY

To be concerned only with making money is the first step to being overtaken by fear. Happiness lies not in the mere possession of money; it lies in the joy of achievement and in the thrill of creative effort.

In today's world money is overvalued. Never let it rule you. A perceptive person should have the energy and rules of money in their head but not in their heart.

None of us actually owns the money that passes through our lives, so our obligation is to use it creatively and responsibly.

Many people believe money and success are the same thing. Yet they are not. Money is a neutral force that merely responds to your will. We all need money in order to conduct our lives, but we do not need to be slaves to money or to crave excess. Nor do we need to live our lives in fear of losing money or not having enough.

A man or a woman is a success if he or she gets up first thing in the morning and goes to bed at night and in between does what he or she wants to do and feels at peace with the role that money has in his or her life.

If the emotional energy behind money does not affect and influence your moods and stability, then your attitude to money is healthy.

There is only one true experience of success – to be able to spend your life in your own way knowing without hesitation that you are living in accord with your inner truth.

And that you are using your money, however much you have, for good things.

An Invocation to Understand Money: The Precious Jewel

This invocation teaches you a deeper understanding of prosperity, achievement and money, while creating the inner power to overcome material obstructions. It is very simple and highly effective.

For best results repeat it at the same time each day over a thirteen-day period. Try to do it in the morning as early as possible; it is most effective when performed at sunrise. It is a very simple invocation and all you need to do is to repeat the words below and, when finished, clap your hands together loudly and slowly thirteen times to secure the energy you have made. Thirteen is regarded as a very lucky number in the Bön tradition, and thirteen is a number of material abundance within these ancient teachings.

> I offer respect and homage
> To all living things,
> For they have come
> From great abundance and
> Shall return to it.
> I offer up my strong mind to be
> Blessed and made pure
> By the first light of the rising sun
> Whose dazzling rays purify and
> Make new all things.
>
> The light of the sun of the new day flows through me,
> A fire of gold, silver and all precious things
> Whose light destroys my financial obstructions! Bring to me now

And throughout the day, treasures, wealth, money
And the wisdom to know how to use it.
For in the essence of living beings lives the precious jewel of life
Endless, constant, abundant, pure,
The ever-present creation of life.

All prosperity comes to me,
Burnt upon my being
By the sun's first rays,
All poverty is cleared from me
By the sun's great heat, never to return,
I shall bring achievement of all good things,
Of soul, the body and the daily mind
Into the household and the hearts of all I meet,
For they shall share in my good fortune.

Money comes to me
And stays the rest of my days . . .
Value calls to me, bringing me insight,
Foresight, patience and thrift.
My heart is made still,
Serene in humility
Before all abundance
That lives in all things.

FINDING SERENITY

In all your activities seek the constant stream of serenity that
supports the material cycles of this fragile world. Stop, be
still and listen to the beauty that sings quietly in all material activities. As you do, give thanks for everything and to
all things.

Know that all true prosperity comes to you through your thoughts and actions if you embrace serenity. The more people who are prosperous in this way, the greater the prosperity for everyone.

Conclude each day as serenely as you can and be finished with it. Leave it behind you as you walk towards the night. As the sun goes down, let your day and all that you have done fade away into the evening. Keep only the spirit of what you have created during the day and allow it to merge with your soul, so that as you rise in the morning, your mind has been imbued by the dynamic force of your own creativity.

Our lives are transient impulses of mental and physical energy, and if we learn how to assemble them, then we shall have neither failure or success, fear or lack of fear, but connection to serenity and ongoing, endless love.

All his life Dorian had battled with success and failure, poverty and prosperity. He made a lot of money, then lost it all and had to start again. The same thing happened with his relationships, reputation, security and wellbeing. He would gain, lose and start again.

Dorian became sick of the up and down rollercoaster of his life. He was tired of trying to prove himself, grasping at what he felt was success and then losing it again. He wanted stability and consistency, but above all he wanted to simply feel content.

Dorian was ready to make changes but unsure of how to go about it. I suggested he practise both the Meditation on Discovering and Strengthening Inner Worth and the Precious Jewel Invocation, while at the same time creating a calmer, less frantic and driven lifestyle for himself.

With this blueprint Dorian began to make small changes. He shortened his working hours, got more exercise and sleep and meditated regularly. This led him to reflect on what he really felt about success and failure. He realised how all his choices and decisions were driven by fear of failure, yet because his inner worth was low, he felt unable to hold on to any success he found.

As Dorian strengthened his sense of inner worth, his values altered. He found the secure life he wanted in a warm relationship, a modest home, a sufficient income and a satisfying job working with young people.

10

SERENITY IN DAILY LIVING

Serenity is simple: it is contentment in all things and happiness with the small things of life, knowing that great and small are the same essential pulse of consciousness. This is serenity in action, in the quiet expression of life, in knowing your life's passage, in delighting in the great mystery and discovering that although in the end there is no mystery, the experience of serenity is both reverential and mysterious.

This is the place within us where beauty always grows, unstoppable and eternal. From this come great inner blessings. It is in the surrender to serenity that we become most human.

Serenity is not so much a state of mind but more of a state of being. It is not dependent on knowing things but on being truly at ease with your heart, mind and body and all their interactions.

You are truly rich, having all that you need when simply, without fuss, you have peace of mind. You then discover the experience of doing nothing while doing everything. In doing nothing, you can create the most memorable moments in life.

Serenity in small things is more important than an impersonal universal serenity because by experiencing serenity in small things, you know and understand that in the course of time and evolution, both fleeting and impermanent, all things are nothing without serenity.

SERENITY IN THE WORLD

During the coming years our world will change in many ways. Many of its resources are running out, and things will change in the physical structure of the planet, as well as in most societies on Earth. We are witnessing the start of the shift from the industrial and economic age to the first impulses of the compassionate age in which businesses, governments and individuals are gradually moving towards responsible and individual development.

This is the century in which the structures of inequality will be revealed both within each person and in the world at large. This is the century where love becomes a necessity, the language of survival. The fear that has gripped us for so long will evolve into love. And the more people who are rooted in serenity, the faster this will happen.

The action of self-healing, which is brought about when we learn serenity, is crucial to the transformation of fear both within ourselves and the world. Because of the lessons the world has begun to learn, this new century will eventually become more harmonious and so less harmful.

Compassion, the seed of peace, will be able to flourish. Let us all be very hopeful. At the same time every one of us has a responsibility to help encourage our global family in the right direction.

Pleasant words and hopes by themselves are not adequate; we must take up the responsibility for what is going on by living our lives as best we can and doing small things each day to shift the balance of change. These small actions then build momentum, so creating immense human change that arises from individual human inventiveness and spiritual awakening.

The actions we must take are both internal and external. We must love and care for our environment, other people and ourselves.

Each of us can help and inspire our fellow human beings profoundly by developing serenity, having the courage to heal fear in ourselves and trusting the dynamic force of our own unselfish inspiration to be of service to others. Individuals can and do make a change in society once they travel beyond their fears. Times of great change, just like this current one, come seldom in human history. It is up to each of us to make the most skilful use of our time, to help create a happier world, where fear no longer beats its doom-laden drum and serenity is the language of all people's hearts.

FIND YOUR PATH

Do not simply walk blindly along the path you are on. Pause to examine with discretion and with love where the path may lead and where the choices you have made in life have taken you.

If you are brave, inspired by your inner love, set out where there is no path, make your own and leave a trace so that others may also find their own path. They need not step in your footsteps, but may walk alongside you with encouragement.

In creating your own path through life, you bring about your own inner teaching and this leads to serenity.

Even if you follow a religious or spiritual and philosophical belief, you must make your own path within that and work to remove any inequality that you find within that belief system.

More than ever before we live in a time of change. This new century we have begun is the century of individual responsibility and individual path-making. As we tread our paths, some of us succumb to fear and some of us fight back. Yet we often fight back with the energy of fear and not with the energy of love. Fighting back against the problems of life inspired by fear brings more fear into your life. If you can love your fear, then it transforms itself into a powerful, sometimes fierce, love that will help you overcome all obstacles, for when you bring love into your life, you have more love available at every moment of your life. The energy of love is serenity and it makes us rich.

MEDITATION

The single greatest tool at our disposal in transforming fear into love and serenity is meditation.

Throughout this book I have offered many different brief meditations for specific purposes, and I hope that some of these may have been of use or value to you. But now I would like to advocate the practice of a daily meditation as the single most life-enhancing act possible in the busy stream of our lives.

Meditation has no specific purpose, though it brings with it an enormous number of benefits. Essentially, meditation simply is and is simply about being. Practising meditation is not the same as practising golf, chess or the violin. It is not something to do to become better at or to add to the chores on your list. Meditation is the act of regularly taking a brief span of time for pure and simple existence. If you practise it as something to learn or improve at, then you are not meditating. This is why meditation is so powerful an ally in healing fear. Fear believes that you should always have a purpose. Meditation is without purpose, without a 'right way' and without any sense of time.

In meditation a faster way of learning is of no importance whatsoever, because one's focus is always on the present. And although growth does occur in the process, it is growth in the same way that a plant grows. This is the essential impulse of meditation.

In meditation you simply observe what is going on, whatever that happens to be. And as you do, fear will fade.

When you listen with intention to a piece of music, you follow the sounds and eventually you understand the music. The point cannot be explained in words because music is not words, but after listening for a while, you understand the point of it, and that point is the music itself.

In exactly the same way, as you meditate, you can listen to all experiences, because experiences of any kind are patterns of light, sound, form and consciousness arising within you. You are these patterns, and if you feel what is happening, the awareness you have of you and of everything else is all the same.

Sight, emotion, touch, smell, taste, memory, sound – all of these unite and are fused as one, all the senses are made complete, and you become a pattern of consciousness creating itself, a picture of what you are and can be. This goes on for ever, whether you are aware of it or not, for this is life flowing through you; life that has no fear and comes from serenity.

Instead of asking what you should do about something, you experience it, because who knows what to do about it? To know what to do about this, you would have to know everything, and if you don't, then the only way to begin is to observe.

Observe not only what's going on outside but also what's going on inside. Treat your own thoughts, your reactions, your emotions about what's going on outside as if those inside reactions were also outside things.

Now, you may say that this is difficult, and that observing what is going on is far more challenging than being busy, and perhaps even that it bores you. But if you wish to experience meditation and the blessings that it brings, then, difficult or not, simply begin.

Sit quite still and observe what is happening: all the sounds outside, all the different shapes and lights in front of your eyes, all the feelings in your body as well as your thoughts, memories, regrets, hopes, fears and needs. As you observe, do not linger, judge or analyse, simply notice these feelings as they pass by.

MINDFULNESS

Mindfulness is one of the qualities that you are migrating towards throughout life, whether you are conscious of this or not. It is the development of compassion and serenity and the regular practice of meditation will develop this quality in you more effectively than any other method.

As you open yourself, through meditation, to the full range of experiences within your consciousness, you become aware of what you perceive in each moment. As a result you no longer deny certain feelings while clinging to others. By coming to know your own pain, you create a bridge to the pain and experience of other people. This enables you to move out of the state of self-absorption, born of fear, and offer help to others. When you understand how it feels to suffer, you become naturally inspired to live a life that does not harm others, or any form of life. You live a life that affirms life and does not harm.

With the compassion and serenity that is mindfulness acting as a bridge to those around us, a true kindness arises within. Knowing that someone will suffer if we perform a harmful action or say a hurtful word, we do these things less often. It is a very simple, natural and heart-full response. Rather than seeing kindness as a set of rules, we experience kindness as an unrestricted reluctance to cause suffering. Kindness is the celebration of love in the expression of the material world.

When our minds become imbued with an understanding of how suffering feels and fill with a compassionate urge not to cause more of it, we naturally recoil from causing harm. In Bön teachings an image is used to reflect this quality of mind: a tuft of hair, held near a flame, instantly curls away from the heat. This happens without self-consciousness or self-righteousness as a natural expression of the heart. For in that moment of discovery you will find that your consciousness greets you as though you have finally come home to the place where you should truly be.

The Two Qualities of Mindfulness

Two qualities are traditionally attributed to this beautiful and delicate sense of consciousness that gives rise to harmlessness: they are described within the Tibetan Bön tradition as 'honourable disgrace' and 'honourable fear'. These qualities have nothing to do with fear or disgrace in an insecure way. They have more to do with a natural and total desire not to cause harm. Honourable disgrace comes from a feeling of disquietude at the possibility of hurting others or ourselves. Honourable fear comes in the form of an unwillingness to cause pain in others because you know in yourself how that feels. In this way opening to your own suffering is the first step in making a deep connection with others. We open to this pain not in order to become down in the dumps or feel miserable but for what it has to offer us. When you find the courage and personal power not to harm and hurt, you are understanding that you, like all other human beings, are not alone and can never be alone.

Sometimes you can be afraid to open up to something painful because it seems as though it will eat you up. However, mindfulness can never be overcome by whatever is the current object of awareness. If you are aware of a troubled and fearful state of mind, the mindfulness within you is not troubled nor is it fearful. Even the most painful emotional or mental state, or extreme physical pain, cannot interrupt and alter mindfulness.

In our culture we are taught to push away, to avoid our feelings. This kind of aversion is the action of a mind caught in separation. Whether in the active, fiery form of anger and rage, or in a more inward, frozen form like fear, the primary function of these mental states is to separate us from what we are experiencing. But the only way that we can be free from suffering ourselves and avoid doing harm to others is by connection – a connection to our own pain and, through awareness and compassion, a connection to the pain of others. We learn not to create separation from anything or anyone. This is mindfulness; this is compassion and serenity.

THE EIGHTEEN VIRTUES

Sometimes our minds, our hearts and our energy can seem like muddy water, but if muddy water is left to rest and be still, it will eventually clear. In the creation of this clarity, which is serenity, you will experience what is called, in the Bön tradition, the Eighteen Virtues. Each of them and all of them will bring serenity into your daily living as they appear naturally in your life. You will not have to make them happen; in fact, you may have some of them already. Once they all appear, you will discover that they enable the serenity within you to be expressed directly into the material world. Read each of them and their descriptions aloud, taking your time, and consider them as you hear yourself speak.

1. BALANCE

Balance comes of its own accord when you start to apply gentle discipline to your speech, thoughts and actions. This then teaches you how all the different parts of your life, body and mind are connected and perfectly balanced.

2. A SENSE OF PURPOSE

When you have balance, you gain a sense of purpose. You will know what you are here to do and why and how. From this point you will create a directed material reality that is also full of spontaneity.

3. A LACK OF SELF-IMPORTANCE

You have no need of self-importance in anything that you think, say or do. You are in accord with the natural cycles. You are like the seasons and have no need to impose your will upon anything. You are yourself in the most divine way you can be.

4. NATURALNESS

You are natural in all your needs. Health and wellbeing are your clothes, and your needs are few, yet you are able to use the energy of all aspects of human experience without prejudice.

5. EFFORTLESSNESS

All things come to you without a struggle, for you know the nature of accomplishment and that is based upon a sure acceptance of your faculties.

6. TRUTHFULNESS

In all things you experience truth and *are* truth, the truth of darkness and of light. People are awakened to their inner truth by the power and conviction of your own truth. You know that there is no refuge in truth, but that it is a path to understanding.

7. ELEGANCE

You are elegant in mind, body, character and actions. Not elegant of the world but of the spirit. All things work in concord with your thoughts.

8. STABILITY

You are stable, strong within yourself, unmoveable. People around you feel that they can pause to catch a breath, to reflect, for you have these aspects as part of your stability.

9. GOOD CHARACTER

You follow your inner calling to know yourself, regardless of what the world may think, and you move beyond its illusions, yet know how to use them. You reflect the character of others. Your character emanates goodness and fairness.

10. FULFILMENT

You know your own fulfilment, you know why, and you live it as a perfect expression. You naturally live by example, without the need to discuss it.

11. MODESTY

You are modest in your nature and express purity in all that you do. Your modesty is empowered by true innocence, which is tough wisdom.

12. PERSISTENCE

You do not give up; for you are sure of the right course of action before you undertake any endeavour.

13. JOYFULNESS

Joy is in all that you do, and in the light of your natural joyfulness other people become joyful too.

14. GRACIOUSNESS

You are kind, accommodating, forgiving but never walked over by other people. You are in love with life, and the whole world can see the passion and intensity of this life-long affair. People are at rest in your presence.

15. GENEROSITY OF SPIRIT

You are truly generous because that is the way of the natural world. You are generous with what you have, and your generosity can never be abused and is always returned.

16. TOLERANCE

You are tolerant of all things and everyone, and through your tolerance others learn tolerance and witness the power of compassion.

17. GOODWILL

You experience boundless goodwill from people, and you express goodwill to others. It is the basis of all your communication. You are always blessed by goodwill, for your goodwill blesses the souls of others.

18. SIMPLICITY

You have no need of excess or superficial trimmings. Whatever your station in life, you live simply, create simplicity and make clear the meaning of your life to yourself. Complications and entanglements do not fill your thoughts and actions. Life is simple.

Each of these eighteen dwells within you as living potential, and as each is awakened, they merge to create a complete serenity that not only empowers you spiritually but also acts as a tool that will enable you to love and live more skilfully.

THE MEANING OF LIFE

If you do not know the meaning of life, do not worry, just live it, for this is the way to give life meaning. Knowing the meaning of life is not crucial to living it. Learn to get in touch with the serenity within yourself and know that everything in this life has a purpose, even if at first the purpose is hidden. Even if you do not know what the purpose is immediately, in your serenity you will find it and by doing so, discover your own. The purpose of life is not that a thing has a function but that it has a meaning, a meaning that inspires you to capture the impulse of life and have it burn within you, conscious and awake, for ever.

You will find, if you are willing, that you carry not just the questions about life but the answers inside you. You will find that profound serenity, which is understanding and acceptance, is all around you: in your home, at your place of employment, on the way to work, in the shower, in your garden and even in a time of conflict or hardship.

Serenity lives as a life force in all things, in a flower, rock, in the very atoms that make matter. It dwells in time, space and in all dimensions.

Serenity dwells within those whom you love and those whom you hate. In the presence of serenity, your soul finds the path to a clearer light, and all things that seem elusive or deceptive are reduced to the shining clarity of extreme gentleness.

Life is a fleeting and sometimes difficult search for meaning, serenity and understanding. Go with serenity in the discovery of your dreams. Live the life you have had the courage to dream of.

And know that in your search for meaning, as you simplify your life, the laws of the universe will become simpler in how they influence you and in what you understand about them.

Most people are subjective toward themselves and objective toward all others. The challenge is to be serenely objective toward oneself and serenely subjective toward all others. The person who can stand alone in the world, only taking counsel from their conscience, lives in a natural state of serenity.

This aspect of serenity directs each of us to the deepest experience of life, an experience that gathers us up and smoothes out our fears, showing us the very consciousness that makes us. Life becomes our friend, and we know finally, once and for all, that life is not a problem to be solved but a reality to be experienced. Life has its own hidden forces, which you can only discover by living.

MORALITY AND GOODNESS

In experiencing and expressing serenity, be good in your heart but do not allow your heart to be overly moral and rigid, so that you miss the fire in life.

Goodness and morality are two different things. Morality adheres to rigid instructions and rules, while goodness knows the nature and rightness of all things and acts accordingly. Goodness can frighten those bound by morals, for it is a hugely powerful force rooted in serenity and the greatest destroyer of fear. If you adhere to any rigid moral code without true goodness in your heart, you may cheat yourself of much of life.

Instead, rise above the two-faced morality of the world; to the unique inner code of your highest consciousness. Do not be good just for the sake of it; be good because serenity fills your life with compassion.

Do not rush to change others. If you wish to convince someone to change their life and see that they are unskilful in their thoughts and actions, then do not try to persuade them but rather practise skilful thoughts and actions yourself. People believe what they see with their hearts, and in this way you create serenity in the world.

WALK TO THE MUSIC OF YOUR HEART

To live with peace of mind, ease and acceptance requires serenity in the living of your life from day to day.

Love and serenity go hand in hand, healing and transforming all obstacles, no matter what or who they are. There is no other way to understand love but to love more. In loving as much as you can, so serenity will increase. As the power of love heals all things, so the power of serenity brings complete and utter understanding of your own life and of other people's. In this understanding there are no obstacles. All things become and are complete.

Let yourself walk to the music of your heart, which you can always hear, when you are in the state of serenity, however far away it may appear to be. Remember that you were born knowing that you are the creator of your own delight and in that delight you will find kindness and know that kindness is the only investment that never fails.

Remember too that all things are, in their essence, at agreement and in harmony, with a unity and a bond of trust, regardless of how things may appear to be. All things are in accord.

In times of discord and frustration your serenity will show you how to release inner accord and trust, so that the hardship and discord will cease and peace and contentment will take the place of negativity. When you are connected to your own serenity, you know how to reveal and release the harmony of things, even when others cannot see a way forward.

Ultimately the simple things in life will bring you happiness. These are the enduring things of life. They are the markers, the strong posts, to which you can tie the threads of serenity that you weave from your heart. They purify you.

You will find that if you examine what they truly are, they will be few. They might include friendship, beautiful music, listening to the rain. They are yours and special to you. These are your important human experiences in which you can ground your serenity so that it will grow and stay strong. When the world seems demanding and everyone is on top of you, look to these markers of serenity to help you access the inner and endless serene state. In knowing serenity, life becomes simple.

Serenity is the body of love that makes life.

Do you have the courage to surrender to that body of love, so becoming the soul that inhabits life?

This is the essence of serenity.

For further information on Christopher Hansard and his work please contact:

Stephen Stokes
General Manager at
SWS@edenmedicalcentre.com

or

www.edenmedicalcentre.com
www.bonmedicine.com
www.bonmedicine.co.uk
www.christopherhansard.com

INDEX

 HODDER MOBIUS

Transform your life
with Hodder Mobius

For the latest information on the best in
Spirituality, Self-Help,
Health & Wellbeing and Parenting,

visit our website
www.hoddermobius.com